Superior Tapestry:

Weaving the Threads of Upper Michigan History

By Deborah K. Frontiera

Modern History Press

Ann Arbor, MI

Learn more at www.SuperiorTapestry.com

Published by
Modern History Press
5145 Pontiac Trail
Ann Arbor, MI 48105

www.ModernHistoryPress.com
info@ModernHistoryPress.com

Tollfree 888-761-6268
FAX 734-663-6861

Contents

Table of Figures..iii

    Superior Tapestry Sites in the Keweenaw................................ v

    Superior Tapestry Sites in the Greater U.P. vi

Introduction-From the Author...vii

Chapter 1 – Birch Bark Canoe...1

Chapter 2 – *Bahweting*: The Sound of the Rapids 11

Chapter 3 – A Bell Tolls 19

Chapter 4 – Fox River Flowing 25

Chapter 5 – One Piano's Plinking..33

Chapter 6 – Portrait of Pictured Rocks.....................................43

Chapter 7 – A Plum Assignment: Sand Point Lighthouse...........49

Chapter 8 – Ring 'Round the Ages 55

Chapter 9 – A Failure in Forging Iron 65

Chapter 10 – Saturday Sauna 71

Chapter 11 – In Bishop Baraga's Footprints 79

Chapter 12 – Chip of the Pines Casino 89

Chapter 13 – Tools of the Home Speak.....................................97

Chapter 14 – The Quincy Mine Man Car................................105

Chapter 15 – A Bridge Across 115

Chapter 16 – The Lady Be Good 125

Chapter 17 – A Stone's Story...135

Chapter 18 – At the Corner of 7ᵗʰ and Elm 145

Chapter 19 – Piles of Poor Rock 153

Chapter 20 – Chrysler Calamity on the *City of Bangor* 161

Chapter 21 – A Tree's Tale 167

Chapter 22 – Fireside Stories of Hearth and Home 173

Chapter 23 – Famous Float Copper 181

Chapter 24 – Toppling Timber 187

Chapter 25 – Daily Happenings at the Ironwood Depot 199

Chapter 26 – Iron Mountain's Monster Pump 205

Chapter 27 – Menominee's Memory: The "Dudly Bug" 211

Appendix – Resources and for Further Reading 219

    Acknowledgements 222

    About the Author 223

    Special offer for readers who visit at least 12 of the sites mentioned in this book: 224

    My Superior Tapestry Logbook 225

Index 227

Note: comprehensive maps of the sites mentioned in this book can be found on pages *v – vi* immediately following the Table of Figures.

Table of Figures

Fig. 1-1: Birch Bark (B.B.) Canoe 1

Fig. 2-1: St. Mary's Rapids 11

Fig. 3-1: *Edmund Fitzgerald* ship's bell...................................19

Fig. 3-2: Whitefish Point Museum Signage 24

Fig. 4-1: The Fox River near where M-28 flows through the town of Seney...25

Fig. 5-1: A Player Piano..33

Fig. 6-1: Pictured Rocks National Lakeshore............................44

Fig. 7-1: Sand Point Lighthouse..49

Fig. 7-2: Sand Point Lighthouse – Fresnel Lens........................54

Fig. 8-1: Rings engraved with "HIS" 55

Fig. 9-1: Signage at Michigan Iron History Museum 65

Fig. 9-2: Overlook at Michigan Iron History Museum 66

Fig. 9-3: The Iron History Museum (2020) 70

Fig. 10-1: Sauna at the Hanka Homestead 71

Fig. 10-2: Hanka Homestead Grounds 77

Fig. 11-1: Statue of Bishop Baraga..79

Fig. 12-1: a $1.00 casino chip from The Pines 89

Fig. 12-2: Baraga County Historical Museum on a summer day (2020) 95

Fig. 13-1: Copper Range Historical Museum Objects................97

Fig. 13-2: More Objects from the museum 104

Fig. 13-2: Copper Range Historical Museum (2020)...............104

Fig. 14-1: The Man Car today..105

Fig. 14-2: The Man Car, filled with men going down for their shift 106

Fig. 15-1: New Bridge (right) and Old Bridge (left) 115

Fig. 15-2: 1st Bridge Between Houghton and Hancock 116

Fig. 15-3: Portage Lake Lift Bridge in the "down" position......123

Fig. 15-4: Portage Lake Lift Bridge in the middle position........123

Fig. 16-1: Propeller from *The Lady Be Good* 125

Fig. 16-2: B-24 in action..133

Fig. 17-1: the former St. Anne's Church 135

Fig. 18-1: *Societa Italiana di Mutua Beneficenza* 145

Fig. 18-2: Memorial Park monument 151

Fig. 19-1: A Pile of Poor Rock...153

Fig. 19-2: Keeweenaw National Historical Park Headquarters.156

Fig. 19-3: Poor rock as a foundation element 158

Fig. 19-4: Migrating sands at Grand Traverse Bay 160

Fig. 20-1: A 1927 Chrysler from the *City of Bangor* 161

Fig. 20-2: City of Bangor..162

Fig. 21-1: Estivant Pines Sanctuary...................................167

Fig. 22-1: Officers' Quarters at Fort Wilikins State Historical Park 173

Fig. 23-1: Replica of the Ontonagon Boulder 181

Fig. 23-2: Another example of float copper 186

Fig. 24-1: Cross-cut saw at Ontonagon County Historical Museum 188

Fig. 25-1: Ironwood Railroad Depot 199

Fig. 25-2: Ironwood Depot (2020) 203

Fig. 26-1: Chaplin Mine Steam Pump................................206

Fig. 27-1: Dudly Bug 211

Fig. 27-2: Dudly's workshop 213

Fig. 27-3: Dudly Universal Frame Jig.................................214

Fig. 27-4: Dudly patent on device for supporting and truing wheels 215

Fig. 27-5: Dudley bugs are Being Used In Great European Struggle 216

Superior Tapestry Sites in the Keweenaw

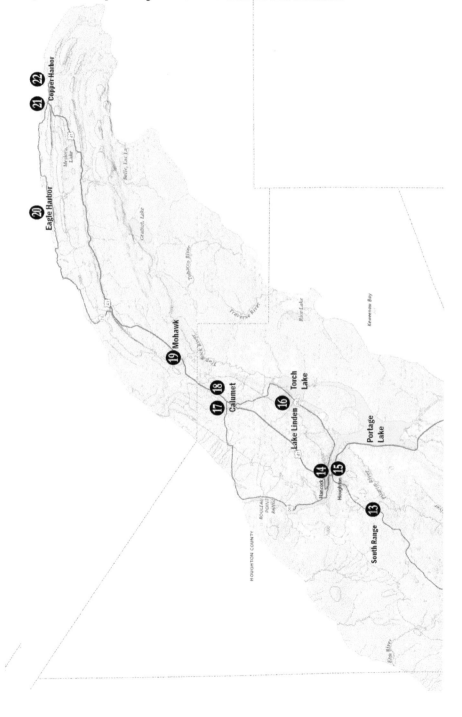

Superior Tapestry Sites in the Greater U.P.

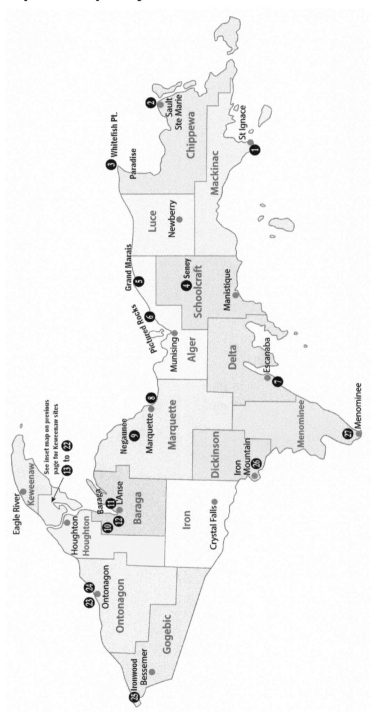

Introduction-From the Author

This book is the result of a conversation with Tony at Copper World in Calumet, Michigan. Tony and I have done business for a number of years, and in the summer of 2019, he asked me when I was going to write a new "Michigan book" for him to stock in his gift shop. I said I'd been writing other things and hadn't thought much about it. He asked what kind of things, and I told him about my novella (a very short novel), *Midnight in the Pawn Shop*. "Hey, why don't you do something like that with things all over the U.P.?" he asked.

My first reaction was to swirl my finger around in little circles and then point to my head—I didn't need any more ideas added to all those already rattling around in my brain. But the thought continued to nag me, so one day, I sat and brainstormed a list of possible "things" in the U.P. that I could "bring to life." Within ten minutes, I had listed over twenty!

Once a good idea gets hold of me, it won't go away, haunting my dreams until I do it. So, Tony, here's your idea brought to life after many hours of research, drafting, writing and rewriting. May you and my readers enjoy the result, *Superior Tapestry*. May you imagine the "lives" of other places and things as you visit my native Yooper Land from Ironwood to Sault Ste. Marie and from Copper Harbor to Menominee.

As I did with *Midnight in the Pawn Shop*, the artifacts, trees, rocks and rivers tell the stories from their points of view. I brought them to life in the hope that the stories they tell will draw my readers more completely into the experience.

While doing research for this book, I found that there are several ways to spell some of the Ojibwa place names, including the spelling of "Ojibwa" itself. If, as a reader, you find that some of the spellings are different from those you know, please don't be upset. I've at least tried to be consistent across my own work. A list of references has been provided in the Appendix.

I also met (by phone and online) many fascinating, knowledgeable and helpful people all across the U.P., who assisted with research, provided helpful links to web sites and contributed their own expertise as historians and writers. This book would not be what it is without them. Many thanks to all of you listed in the Appendix.

Note on photos: Most of the photographs in this work were taken by the author. Other archival and personal photos are credited in the Acknowledgments section at the end of this book.

Chapter 1 – Birch Bark Canoe

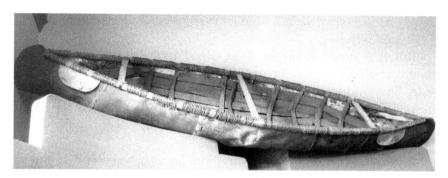

Fig. 1-1: Birch Bark (B.B.) Canoe

You will need to look up to see the Birch Bark (B.B.) Canoe in the Museum of Ojibwa Culture in Saint Ignace, Michigan. You'll see many other fascinating artifacts there, too.

The great sturgeon slides swiftly and gracefully through the water. Ojibwa legends say that it inspired the shape of their canoes. Using a canoe is much faster than walking, so that's how the Ojibwa liked to travel. Lakes and rivers were their highways because forest paths were hard to walk on and went up and down mountains.

To ensure they would last many years, canoes were carefully built and looked after.

One winter, the wind howled and blew the trees, day after day. The old birch tree had swayed and stood tall through many such blizzards, but she was old and weak now. A mighty gust struck her, and she fell flat between two trees in the forest behind her. She hoped she would turn into soil to feed new birch seedlings, even though she knew that would take many years. She had seen Ojibwa women carry baskets made of birch bark when they came to pick berries in summer, so she knew they might come to strip her bark. Birch Bark, or B. B. as she liked to call herself, knew that birch bark, was good for many things, including stopping fungus from spoiling food stored in such a basket.

When the snow melted, she was exposed and awoken by the cut of a stone axe. It hurt as it split B.B. down the length of her trunk, but the wedges prying B.B. away from the rest of the log seemed to free her to a new life.

The men walked heel to toe, counting. When they reached eighteen, they nodded. One said, "Good. We can make this new canoe from a single log." One of them picked up the long curl of bark and carried her away.

B.B. managed to whisper, "Goodbye" to the rest of the tree as the man carried her across the meadow and into the forest on the other side. She wondered what a canoe was. Not long after, she found herself on the ground in the middle of an Ojibwa village. Since it was getting dark, the man who carried her entered his wigwam, which was what they called their houses.

A crow landed on B.B. She knew him because he had often landed on her branches in the forest. "What's a canoe?" she asked him.

"People sit in it and travel over water," Crow said. "This village is close to where the waters of two Great Lakes come together. You will see it in the morning."

Then, he went on to explain that many Native Peoples often got together where Lake Michigan and Lake Huron joined up with narrow strips of water called "straits." Mackinac Island, St. Ignace, and Mackinaw City were all there.

The Ojibwa from the Lake Superior area, the Ottawa from the Lake Michigan region and the Huron People shared many customs. Their languages were also similar, since all three were part of a greater group known as the *Anishnaabe*, or "first man."

They lived from the land, hunting many types of animals. They used tree roots, bark and leaves for medicine, baskets and many other things. In the meadows and marshes, they gathered berries, wild rice and other plants for food, and caught fish in the lakes and rivers. Nothing was wasted, since nearly every part of the animals and plants provided something of use.

"I've watched these people for many years," Crow said. "They are almost as smart as I am. They do some clever things, such as making the birch bark canoes like you will be."

The next morning, two men lay B.B. in a long, narrow trench in the ground. They poured hot water over her to soften her so she could be formed into the shape they wanted. It felt lovely. She was no longer afraid and let herself relax and enjoy this bath. As she soaked, Crow told her that if the water had been cold, she would have had to soak from one full moon until the next.

Here is how they heated water: They made bags from the stomachs of animals they had hunted and filled these with water. They heated stones in a fire, then put the hot rocks and the water sacks in a pit until the water was hot enough.

B.B. watched as the people used other pieces of bark taken from the smaller branches of the birch tree to make many other things: baskets, cups, roof coverings (called "shingles") for wigwams, fans, scrolls for ritual art, and pictorial maps.

B.B. and these objects sometimes smiled at each other from a distance. They never had a chance to speak, since they were all carried inside the lodges once they were complete and B.B. was always outside. Once B.B. was soft from soaking, men drove stakes into the ground in parallel lines to make the canoe the correct width and tied her top edges to these stakes with strips of basswood bark so she would dry in a gently curved shape. Stones anchored the bottom of the curve to the ground.

As B. B. waited to gain a new shape, she watched the men go into the woods again. Crow told her they went to gather other needed supplies, like white cedar, which they would soak and cut into strips for her ribs and rails. Other strips of bark from basswood trees would be used for tying and binding, and thin roots from white or black spruce made perfect twine for sewing.

"I know these trees from their odor, color and texture," B.B. said to Crow.

"All the wood strips and bark have to be soaked like you to make them flexible enough for what they want to do," Crow noted.

B.B. watched women go into the forest, too. The moon had changed from a thin crescent to well past full by the time the People gathered everything they needed. Crow told B.B. he had to leave to help his mate raise their hatchlings.

B.B. was fascinated to listen to a man explain to his son that a tree's roots are the same under the ground as the branches above. So, he looked up, followed a branch and then dug for the root right under it. The father said that they wanted only the thinnest roots near the surface. When they returned from the forest with many roots, he showed his son how to strip the bark of the root away until only a twine-like string, called *watap*, remained. The moon waned, became new, and began to wax once more as the men soaked the roots and worked various timber parts of the canoe into place. The longest was the keel, which went from front to back and would be the backbone of the canoe. There was a handrail, cedar ribs stiffening it side to side, and cedar strips to put their feet and goods carried in the canoe on. They didn't want anything to make a hole in the birch bark hull!

Now it was the women's turn to work on B.B. canoe. They cut the ends to form a curve and began to sew the pieces together. B.B. felt the poke of the pointed bone awl as it made holes in the two parts to be joined, but it didn't hurt. Then, the women wove the *watap* in and out through the holes. That tickled. They also sewed or tied the cedar keel, hand rail, and ribs into place with strips of thicker cedar or basswood bark. This took several days.

B. B. watched as the women brought lumps of raw balsam fir sap back to the camp. She had heard an older woman speak yesterday of scraping it from those trees and placing the sticky stuff into deerskin bags. They hung these bags high enough above the crackling fire to heat them but not so close that the bags were burned. The gum rose to the surface, leaving bits of dirt and bark in the bottom of the bag. They squeezed and stretched the gum until there was no water left and the gum looked like honey. Then, the women added tallow (fat) from the animals hunted by the men and heated the mixture in a bag again to blend it all. This they put into cold water and finally wrung all the water out of it again.

An old woman told her daughter, "This makes sure the resin doesn't shrink or crack in cold water or melt in the hot sun, causing leaks." Finally, the woman demonstrated how to splay the end of an ashwood stick into a brush to paint the resin onto all the seams and holes of B.B. so she would be completely watertight.

When will I be ready to go into the water? B.B. wondered.

It was early fall by the time B.B. was ready for use. Two men carried her into shallow water. Oh, how cold it was! Waves sloshed along B.B.'s sides as she slid around the sheltered bay on the northern shore of Lake Huron. Soon, the water no longer seemed so frigid. One man pointed to an island, now called Mackinac Island, asking if they should go there, but the other shook his head, and they paddled back to shore.

Her first voyages that fall were short, with women paddling her into marshes, where they gathered wild rice. B.B. enjoyed listening to the women chat with each other as they cut stalks of wild rice right at the water's surface and piled bundles of it into B.B.'s curved bottom. Their talk, like that of women everywhere through the ages, involved which young man liked which young woman, whether or not they had gathered and dried enough berries, and now wild rice, to feed their clan through a long, cold winter, and whether the men had caught enough fish (which the women had worked hard to dry or smoke) and hunted enough meat to last the same amount of time.

It seemed to B.B. that all of the warm months had been spent preparing for the cold ones. She understood this. Did not the tree she had come from do the same thing? All the trees soaked up summer sun, warm air and rain to produce extra sweet sap, sent down for storage in their roots. In the spring, that sap would rise to feed the tree until new leaves grew from buds to make more food for the tree.

Once the rice harvest was over, snowflakes began to fall, and the first sheen of ice formed on the lake. B.B. was taken on to shore and turned over to protect her from the many blizzards of winter that would soon come. She slept all winter, just as she had when she was a tree.

One day, B.B. felt rain pouring over her, melting all the snow around. Her friend Crow returned. "No more fishing through holes in the ice for the men. It has broken up."

New leaves formed a green veil on the trees when the men began to take her out onto Lake Huron to fish. When the leaves were nearly fully green, and white flowers with yellow centers bloomed around the camp, two men strange to the clan and to B.B. arrived with some of their southern Huron cousins. The strange men had grizzled hair on their faces and wore clothes not made from the skins of animals. Two Huron paddled the canoe with these strange men in it. They also brought things the People had never seen before.

B.B. could not hear the discussions between the Huron cousins and the leaders of her clan, but the canoe they came in was beached right next to her. "I've come from a place to the south and east of here," this canoe told her. "There are many people there dressed like these two. The Huron people have been trading with them for quite a while, to the benefit of both. Now, these men want to trade with your group and others even farther away."

"What does 'trade' mean?"

"Your group would give these men the furs of animals they hunt in the woods and streams, especially beaver. It seems these people really like the fur of beavers and it is sent even farther away than I have ever been. I see their huge ships on a great river far from here. These ships are many times our size and have long poles sticking up with huge white cloths. The wind blows them where they want to go. Then, these men give your group things like those I carried here for your people to see."

The other canoe called that far-away place the St. Lawrence River. She told B.B. that she had heard that the first contact between Europeans, specifically the French-Canadians and Jesuit missionaries, and Native Peoples in the upper Great Lakes was somewhere around a year they called 1640, perhaps a generation ago.

"What are all these things you brought?" B. B. asked.

The other canoe was glad to show off her knowledge. "The metal kettles with the handles can be hung over a fire to cook food and to heat water. There are axes and knives made of iron. Your people will find them far better than their stone tools—at least the People where I come from think so. There are also beads and trinkets that the women will like."

"But I don't see enough goods for very many people here."

"No, not on this trip. I heard the men say that they hope to show them to all the clans of people along these lakes. They hope to invite them to come to the opposite shore next spring, with many furs for your people to trade for all the things they want. They are hoping a couple of men from your village will go with them and introduce them to other clans."

"What a wonderful adventure! I hope I am chosen to go with you."

When the elders of the clan, the Huron Cousins, and the two strange men came out of the meeting lodge, everyone was smiling. The women admired the kettles, commenting on how much easier heating water and cooking would be with these. The women also admired the beads and trinkets. The men picked up the knives and axes and exclaimed about how sharp they were. The strange men invited them to try them out and talked about how many furs they should give to receive a kettle, knife or axe.

The clan chief pointed out two good men to paddle with the others and then pointed to B.B. "This is our newest and best canoe. Take it."

B.B.'s heart nearly burst in excitement.

Early the following morning, they left the village and paddled eastward to a narrow channel between the mainland and a large island, arriving in late afternoon. They could have gone farther before dark, but there were Ojibwa villages both on the mainland and the island, inhabited by people the traders wanted to talk to.

These clans also smiled and approved of the trade goods—even speaking to each other of the greater effort they would put forth in hunting beaver between then and the following spring. The clans said they knew of the place where the big meeting would happen and would come to share in the exchange of gifts.

The next morning, they didn't leave early, since they only planned to travel as far as *Bahweting of Gitchi Gumi Sipe,* where they would have to portage, or carry, the canoes along the shore around the rapids of what the fur traders would later name the St. Mary's River. Many clans would meet there soon for a summer festival, so they would stay several days and be able to feast and talk. Other canoes full of people from their own clan would be joining them for the celebration and then return to their village, while B.B. and the same two paddlers would travel on with the traders.

Family groups arrived at the festival on different days, but nobody minded. B.B. knew that it was just after the new moon when they had arrived at the rapids. She had such a wonderful time listening to the festivities that she hoped she would be paddled to this place every summer for many years to come. The singing, dancing, and eating went on for many days. Every night, while the stars twinkled brightly above, the People sat around great fires and listened to the stories of the past.

B.B. and the other canoes also heard pleasant talk among the clans about the coming gift exchange. Men described the number of days of travel ahead for the traders and some of the dangers along the way. The traders were pleased to hear that since the clans of the Keweenaw had come to the festival that year, they could save two days travel around the point of that peninsula with the short distance they had to portage their canoes around marshes at the two ends of an inner lake.

The moon was past full on the last night of the festival. B.B. was anxious to see the huge lake, *Gitchi Gumi*, which lay above the river. A strong west wind blew that morning, so the group decided to stay near the shore. They camped that night at what would later be called Whitefish Point, where they would be protected from the waves building up in the wind. B.B. heard the French traders give their own name to this largest of the Great Lakes—*Lac Superior*—the lake above. As it turned out, they would remain in the lee, the side protected from the wind, of Whitefish Point for two days, waiting for the wind and waves to return to a safe traveling level. B.B. thought the waves were still too large, but the wind was calm now. The men said these waves were only "rollers" (large rolling waves left after a storm) and paddled on. B.B. saw how her bow cut through the top of each wave and bobbed up and down. The men were right.

It was a full day of hard paddling from there to a safe bay later named Grand Marais. There, they spoke with another clan and rested a day. The clan here said the stretch of shore ahead was sometimes dangerous, going along great sand hills and cliffs with no safe place to land if the wind and waves rose quickly. B.B. gasped when she saw those great hills of sand coming straight down; there was no place to beach a canoe. The cliffs following were even larger. They stopped briefly at the only beach. There, the People offered tobacco to the spirits of the cliffs, asking for continued safe travel. B.B. watched all around for any signs of increasing wind as they passed by colorful cliffs, one of which a Frenchman said looked like a castle. B.B. didn't understand the word.

Once they were safely past the cliffs, another clan met them in a bay protected by a large island. This clan smiled and nodded at the talk of exchanging gifts with the French. Then, it was an easy day's paddle to a safe place (that would later be named Presque Isle), where yet another clan welcomed them. It was such a lovely place, and B.B. wished they had stayed longer.

Their next segment would be their longest paddle yet in one day, all the way to what the French would name "L'Anse," the end of the bay. Good weather favored them as they left during the pre-sunrise light, and they did not arrive until the post-sunset twilight, never stopping even to eat, but paddling with long, hard strokes the whole day. They could have stopped along the way in places where rivers entered Lake Superior providing safe harbors, but chose not to. A cliff at L'Anse, similar to the ones B.B. had seen a few days before—but not nearly so long—dropped off into a flat area with a sandy beach in front of a marsh. They rested a few days and had good meetings with the clans in that area. It had now been nearly one moon since they had left B. B.'s village, and the fur traders spoke well of the journey so far.

The next morning, they woke to cold, drizzling rain. The local clan's elders warned that worse weather might be on the way. So, they decided to stay close to the eastern shore of Keweenaw Bay and got into the safety of the inner lake beyond the marshes as soon as they could. The group turned B.B. and the other canoe over so they would not fill with rainwater. She was glad to stay put for a while—heavy waves made her feel unsteady. It was a good decision, as two days of heavy rain and wind did, indeed, follow. On the third morning, the weather cleared, and they had good paddling through the inner lake. It was a quick haul around a shallow marsh and then back onto *Gitchi Gumi*. It was good paddling all the way to the mouth of the Ontonagon River. The Ojibwa clan there welcomed them and agreed to trade in the coming years, but at that time, they did not take the strange new men up the river to see their great secret. They did, however, send a canoe of their own to show them which islands in a group, later named the Apostle Islands, housed other clans who might like to meet them.

B.B., the men of her clan and the Frenchmen spent two days amid those lovely islands off the shore of what would later be named Bayfield, Wisconsin. One more jaunt took them to the "nose" of Lake Superior and a clan of Ojibwa in the area, now called Duluth, Minnesota. They had been traveling over a month now and decided to rest a few days. B.B. and the other canoes were glad and enjoyed listening to the discussions among the fur traders and the Ojibwa clan elders as they sat around camp fires.

"There are many more clans along the rivers up this shore," B.B. heard, "many days more travel—first north, then east and then south again, much farther than you have already come, before you will circle back to where you began on *Gitchi Gumi*."

Another added, "If you trust us, leave these trade things with us, and we will make the journey at least to the north shore at the head of the lake and as far as Lake Nipigon, telling them of the place of trade you describe."

The Frenchmen nodded.

The following day, they began the journey back along the way they had come. Now, they paddled harder and farther each day, cutting through the middle of the Keweenaw again, but this time heading straight across the bay and beyond. They spent the nights in protected river entrances they found along the way. The weather remained good, so the journey back required only half the time of the trip west.

The home clan welcomed the travelers back after their journey. B.B. had enjoyed her long adventure, but she was glad to be home, too. The women were relieved to have their best canoe back; it was time for the rice harvest. Their Huron cousins left with the two Frenchmen two days later.

B.B. had proven that her people were experts in the art of canoe building. Her hope to be at many summer festivals came to pass. Her adventures would continue over many years for trade, fishing and wild rice harvests.

You can see a replica of Birch Bark Canoe at the Museum of Ojibwa Culture, 500 N. State St., Saint Ignace, Michigan, 49781. It is open Memorial Day to June 30, seven days a week from 9:00 a.m. to 5:00 p.m.; July 1 through Labor Day from 9:00 a.m. to 8:00 p.m. and from Labor Day to Oct. 31, from 10:00 a.m. to 5:00 p.m. Check for any changes in hours or for tours by calling 906-643-9161 or email   ojibmus@lighthouse.net.   Visit www.SuperiorTapestry.com/sites for more info.

Chapter 2 – *Bahweting*: The Sound of the Rapids

Fig. 2-1: St. Mary's Rapids

Photo from the Canadian side of the river during the summer of 2020. Hopefully, you can feel the force of the moving water and hear the sound.

The rivers and lake shores everywhere change over time. This is especially true for Michigan's Upper Peninsula. Over millions and even billions of years, rocks were formed, broken down and turned into rocks again. Earth's Ice Age ended 10, 000 to 12,000 years ago. Thousands of tons of ice pressed down on the surface of the whole of the peninsula. As the ice moved, it scraped away the rock underneath. Also, this was only the last Ice Age of many others that came before. After the glaciers melted, even the shores of *Gitchi Gumi* (Lake Superior) were not the same.

Gitchi Gumi Sipe, the rapids of the St. Mary's River, knew this as she flowed easily, at first, from Whitefish Bay around a curve or two. But then she became shallower and dropped quickly over rocks, tumbling in a way that created great danger for any sort of boat or ship, until she deepened, smoothed out again and wound her way pleasantly down to Lake Huron. Birds flew over her, fish swam up and down her from one lake to the other, with a bit more difficulty going up. The eagles were clever fishing birds, soaring above her and then diving down to grip a fish in their talons when it swam a little too close to the surface. Smaller animals stayed on one side of her or the other; larger ones chose safer places to swim across, away from her swift rapids.

Gitchi Gumi Sipe with her *Bahweting,* the name of the sound of water rushing in the rapids, enjoyed thousands of years with only the wild creatures along her shores and the fish within her to keep her company, but people at last came to her shores. There were only a few at first, and then more and more as the Ojibwa People enjoyed the many fish they caught. They also made use of the plants and animals in the forests and meadows near her shores. Sometimes in the warmer seasons, many Ojibwa gathered along her shores to sing, dance and celebrate things she did not understand. She was good to them because they were good to her, respecting the rapids, where they pulled their canoes to shore. Then they walked, carrying their things to the next safe place where they could paddle again.

Often at these summer festivals, *Bawhweting* heard the elders tell the youngsters stories of their history. She especially liked the story of Waynaboozhoo and the Great Flood. It seemed that the Creator had grown weary of the evil of men and had decided to send a flood to destroy them all – except for one man, Waynaboozhoo, who survived by making a large raft of sticks and other things floating by. On this, he gathered a number of animals to help them survive. If he could just get some mud from the Old World, he was sure he could build a new place for them all to live. When Loon and Beaver were unable to swim down to the Old World to get a bit of mud, Waynaboozhoo asked who else would try. Bahweting heard the Ojibwa tell this tale for generations before she heard a similar story about Noah and his Ark from Jesuit missionaries who came much later.

The Aajigade, a coot (a small diving water bird), offered, but the other animals ridiculed him because he was so small. The other animals argued many hours about how to accomplish the task until it was nearly dark. Then, one of them spotted something floating and they found it was tiny Aajigde. In his beak was a tiny bit of mud. Waynaboozhoo was able to revive him and built a new land from that mud, until it was large enough for Moose to walk about on it!

Bahweting was as entertained as the youngsters sitting around the elder's feet.

She felt these native people were quite clever in the way they caught large numbers of fish. They made nets by curving small branches into a hoop and then weaving thin roots together into a net hanging from the hoop. With these nets, they could scoop up many fish at once, feeding their clan and then hanging more to dry in the summer sun so that they might have food later.

Gradually, the number of people visiting *Gitchi Gumee Sipe* increased and another kind of people appeared. These people dressed differently, had lighter skin and lots of hair on their faces and their heads. They met with the people she had always known to trade or exchange gifts. They, too, had to drag their canoes onto shore and around her rapids. More and more of them came.

These new people were not content to carry only canoes around her rapids. The river heard them call her by a new name: Sault Ste. Marie—"sault" meaning "rapids" and she, as a river, called St. Mary's River. She watched as these light-skinned people presented the Ojibwa with goods—blankets, metal cooking pots, iron tools and other things—they brought from somewhere she did not know. The native people had not been able to make such things from the forest products or animals living there. They had used stones, and sometimes bits of hammered red metal, as they had for hundreds of years, but these things were of much better quality. In exchange, the Ojibwa gave them the furs of animals they hunted in the forests, streams and marshes.

After several years of this trade, a few of the new people—who were dressed even more strangely—arrived. The first, whose name the river did not catch, did not stay long the first year. The river listened as these men in black robes described their religion and tried to persuade the Ojibwa to worship with them. From what Bahweting noticed, the Ojibwa seemed more curious than convinced.

It was some years later, in 1668 (but the river didn't keep track of such things), when three more of these black-robed men arrived. She heard the People call them Claude-Jean Allouez, Claude Dablon, and Jacque Marquette. These men lived with the people, learned their language and tried to help them in many ways. Sometimes, the river watched canoes carry one or two of them over the water to other places she knew not.

Bahweting watched and listened when, in the summer of the human year 1674, a huge number of Ojibwa and French fur traders met to talk and celebrate with great feasts. The river noted that they seemed well pleased with their trading—the Ojibwa liked the improved tools and goods the French brought. The French wanted more and more of the furs of animals that the Ojibwa got for them. More of the men in black robes came, too, and stayed with the Ojibwa people longer and longer. She heard the men in black robes tell the Ojibwa that they should not drink so much of the alcohol the traders gave them in exchange for furs.

More new people came in canoes that were more than twice the size of the native ones, so strong they could be paddled faster, farther and with more in them than ever before. But it took six people to carry the heavier new canoes around Bahweting. They built carts and wagons with wheels to transport more and more bundles of fur, boxes, crates and barrels. They built houses, where they lived all year, not just gathering for summer festivals and then returning to their home villages as the Ojibwa people did. These houses were much bigger than the domed huts built of straight branches covered with bark the river was used to seeing.

Bahweting remained curious but was not sure if she liked these new people. They always wanted more than what they had and seemed to have less patience with her. Over the following years, they began to build ships on the upper side of her rapids, carrying their freight from one ship on the lower end around the rapids to a ship on the upper end. This satisfied them, but only for a time.

They portaged whole ships uphill. She watched and laughed a little, as they greased roads and used capstans—something like a large, upright pulley with a rod inserted to turn it—to pull that huge water craft with ropes, rolling it over logs, pushing, pushing, pulling,

pulling, sweating and grunting to move it around her impassable rapids. It took them three months to move one ship that way. It was the beginning of a fleet of ships on the Lake Superior side of Bahweting to make shipping possible once goods were carried around her.

But these people wanted more. On her eastern side, which she heard them call Canada, they dug a canal around Bahweting. Within the canal, they built a thing strange to her. It was a long, rectangular hole with a gate at each end. They filled it with water and called it a lock. She heard them speak of the year 1797.

Their main idea was to close the gates at each end, pump the water out of the hole to the level of the lower part of the river, have a ship enter, close the gate and pump water in to float the ship up, then open the upper gate so the ship could power its way through the upper part of the river into Lake Superior. For a ship coming down the river, they closed the gates, filled the giant hole with water, opened the upper gate so the ship could enter, drained the water and finally opened the lower gate so the ship could go downstream. The river was in some ways proud of the way they kept working at solving their problem with her rapids. This very first lock around Bahweting allowed for a ship just under thirty-eight feet long to pass more easily and in much less time than ever before.

But in less than fifteen years, the groups of light-skinned people were fighting against each other—Bahweting didn't know the reason—but a small group of men from the American side destroyed that lock so that it could not be used by people called British on the Canadian side. Following that time, the Northwest Fur Company moved a few more ships, using the roller method to increase the number of ships sailing Lake Superior, whose gales and rocks sank many ships over the years. There were so many trading companies that the river stopped trying to remember all the names she heard.

In 1853, Bahweting heard people on the shore talking in great excitement. The United States Congress had granted the state of Michigan 750,000 acres of land to sell to raise money for a new, bigger lock. It would be built 100 feet wide, twelve feet deep and big enough for ships up to 250 feet long and sixty feet wide. The river heard people talking of the formation of a company, the St. Mary's Falls Ship Canal Company. *This ought to be interesting to watch!* Bahweting thought.

Around this same time, Bahweting noticed another of the priests of the light-skinned people, as he stayed from time to time in the growing town of Sault Ste. Marie. This one, whose name she heard was Baraga, tended to both the Ojibwa and the White people, speaking multiple languages with ease. She watched him cross the ice in winter to minister to his people in Canada, as well as those on the American side. He was often gone for long periods of time. She saw how he walked with ease over the snow in snowshoes like those she had seen used in years past by the Ojibwa and the French fur traders. That was still the only way to get around in the winter time, and most people she saw did not go far during the months of snow and ice. But winter didn't seem to bother Baraga, and Bahweting wondered about that. Later, she heard people refer to him as Bishop Baraga, so it seemed he was of some importance. Over one particular winter, she watched as he braved the ice on several occasions to visit sick people on one of the islands along her course.

Bahweting listened and watched something even more interesting, as a man named Charles T. Harvey started work in June of 1853 on that new lock. Men labored to dig a canal on the Michigan side of the river. From spring thaw to late fall ice, an army of workers swarmed over the project. Bahweting noticed that—compared to the earlier canal—they used better tools and machines and did so in more clever ways. As she listened over a two-year period, she learned that the cost rose to $1,000,000. She heard men brag that the entire canal was 5,400 ft. long and 100 ft. wide with not one, but two locks built next to each other, 350 ft. long and seventy ft. wide. Two ships could pass at the same time, one down and one up her course.

Men said each ship paid a toll to go through the locks. Now, more and more ships passed through, from spring thaw to fall freeze, transporting people and much-needed supplies to areas to the west, where iron and copper mines brought underground riches to a world hungry for these raw materials. This hustle and bustle made it much less peaceful along Bahweting's shores. She missed the quiet she had known for so many hundreds of years and could now have only when she froze over during the winter, but she also enjoyed some of the excitement. Humans had, indeed, conquered the problem of getting around her rapids, but Bahweting remained in the center of it all, flowing freely as she always had, fish still quickly swimming down her course and laboring to swim upstream. In later years, fish would also swim up their own canal on the Canadian side.

It seemed like, in only the blink of an eye, the State Locks were no longer enough. Would these people ever rest? By the human year 1881, people turned over the whole lock system to the United States Army Corps of Engineers in order to build more, longer and deeper locks than the State of Michigan could afford on its own. These opened in 1886 and 1896. Bahweting watched and listened over the years as people built the Davis Lock in 1914 (1350 ft. long, 80 ft. wide and 23.1 ft. deep), the Sabin Lock in 1919 (1350 ft. long, 80 ft. wide and 23.1 ft. deep), the McArthur Lock in 1943, (800 ft. long, 80 ft. wide and 31 ft. deep) and the Poe Lock in 19681200 ft. long, 110 ft. wide and 32 ft. deep).

All this was because water was still the cheapest way to transport tons and tons of freight. Bahweting was amazed one day when she heard some people say that a 1000 foot "Laker," a super-sized freighter, carried as much as six 100-car trains, each of which held 10,000 tons, or 2,308 eighteen-wheeler trucks, each of which could hold twenty-six tons! The Canadians had built locks over the years, too.

People also dug canals to produce hydroelectric power, both on her Michigan side and her Canadian side. The cities on both sides of her kept growing, but always, Bahweting remained in the middle of it all, happily bounding over the rocks that had been there for thousands of years.

Still, the changes would continue, and talk began of yet another "super lock" that would allow larger international ships and floating hotel cruise ships to go up and down. Bahweting wondered if it would ever stop and what another hundred years would bring. She knew that nothing could pass between the Lakes Superior and Huron that she did not see.

NOTE: The rapids themselves are best viewed from a park on the Canadian side. See www.SuperiorTapestry.com/sites for more info.

Chapter 3 – A Bell Tolls

Fig. 3-1: *Edmund Fitzgerald* ship's bell

The bell from the *Edmund Fitzgerald* sits enclosed in glass to protect it for generations to come.

Bell didn't remember much about how or where she was cast, but she marked the day she was attached to the top of the wheelhouse on the *Edmund Fitzgerald* as the beginning of her life. Shiny in her newness, Bell understood her job was to ring with the roll of the waves, letting any other water craft know they were close to a huge ore boat. But she wondered why the ship's size and engine noise wouldn't be enough. In the event that water was calm and fog rolled in, someone would ring her to warn others. She knew how important that would be; others depended on her. The man in charge of attaching her gave her one last rub to clean off his fingerprints, then gave her a tap to check her tone. He nodded and smiled. Bell beamed.

Talk around the shipyard the day the *Edmund Fitzgerald* was launched let Bell know that the ore freighter had been named for the president of the board of Northwest Mutual Life Insurance Co. The ship carried on part of the business of that company, a "maximum sized" Great Lakes bulk carrier whose keel had been laid August 7, 1957. Bell had been installed shortly before the launch, on June 8, 1958.

Bell rang happily, clanging with the roll of the waves on Lake Superior and Lake Huron on many voyages, carrying loads of taconite, a low grade of iron ore, from Superior, Wisconsin to the steel mills around Detroit and Toledo. She went through the locks at Sault Ste. Marie many times, raised over twenty feet on the empty voyage upstream and lowered, fully loaded, on the way back down. From her place on top of the wheelhouse, Bell could see far off to the horizon when out of sight of land. Even on that huge a ship, Lake Superior was so vast it made her feel tiny. Her view of fabulous shore lines, the variety of cliffs, rocks, forests and sandy beaches, gave her a sense of awe. Port shores teamed with life and the huge machines of industry, stating that people had conquered the wild, and Bell was part of the world of people.

She watched the crewmembers moving about the deck, closing hatches—clang, bang and clunk—as she left a port fully loaded and opening them for unloading when the ship came near the end of each journey. Often, she viewed pleasure craft far below her: sailboats and cruisers with only a few people aboard, waving as they stayed a safe distance from the huge freighter. Successful trips went on for seventeen years, and the *Edmund Fitzgerald* gave good value to her owners.

On November 9, 1975, the ship was loaded with 26,116 long tons of taconite pellets (marble-size balls of partially-processed iron) at dock #1 in Superior, Wisconsin, bound for Zug Island near Detroit, and set to depart at 2:30 p.m. Bell listened to two crew members just below her. "Going to get some heavy weather this time," said the first.

"Yes, but we'll be traveling close to the *Anderson*, out of Two Harbors, Minnesota. Captain McSorley and Captain Cooper plan to travel fairly close together and in constant radio contact."

"Yeah, you're right; we'll be fine. Captain McSorley said, just to be on the safe side, that he decided to take a more northerly route, closer to Isle Royale than to the Keweenaw and then head down to Whitefish Point."

Rollers made Bell *ding* and *dong* gently as they left port. She wasn't worried. Gales in November were common on Lake Superior, but the worst usually came later in the month. Besides, Bell knew that Captain McSorley and the *Anderson's* captain were both experienced sailors, who knew what Lake Superior could dish out. They knew each other from other trips, and she once heard them talk easily on the deck below her. The lee side (the side away from the wind) of Whitefish point provided some protection when strong winds blew from the north or west, a natural breakwater at the edge of that bay. If the wind blew from the east, then there was no protection, but the worst gales came from the north or west. Early in the voyage, Bell watched the crew double check all the hatches to be sure they were well secured. She knew the phrase "batten down the hatches" as a precaution for heavy weather. Yes, they would be fine.

Gale warnings went up around 7 p.m. on November 9 and were upgraded to storm warnings on November 10. Bell clanged and clanged as the ship rolled in increasingly higher seas. She was not concerned, though, as she had seen weather like this before. She continued to clang, her sound reaching out for miles. But the wind gusts increased to over fifty miles an hour. Waves grew in size from twelve to sixteen feet! Bell remembered what she had heard when she was young about how waves are measured from a flat surface, but there is always a trough and a crest. The distance from the bottom of the trough to the top of the crest is double that of the wave. From dip to top of twelve-to-sixteen-foot waves meant a wall of water twenty-four to thirty-two feet overall—a powerful force of water, lashing against the ship, freezing cold spray flying up to the deck.

Bell clanged unceasingly! Louder and louder!

On November 10, Bell shuddered as the *Edmund Fitzgerald* passed what she considered way too close to a thirty-six-foot shoal (underwater rocks not showing above) near Caribou Island. They'd never gone that close to it before. Bell thought she heard a crunch of the shoal against the bottom of the ship, but she could not be sure. She tried to reassure herself that it wasn't that far before they would reach the safety of Whitefish Point. The rain had turned to snow, and she could no longer see the *Anderson* behind her.

Suddenly, a terrible gust of wind tore a fence rail and two vents from the deck. Bell felt a slight list of the ship, and the tone of her ringing changed with that tilt. It seemed dark as night in the storm, but Bell knew it was only mid-afternoon. Her breath came in huge gulps. The ship slowed down. Ah, a bit of relief. She could see the *Anderson* again.

The noise of the wind and waves now drowned out her clanging. She could hear the pumps through the deck and hull. That meant water was coming into the hold! Bell's tone shook in fear. This was the worst storm she had experienced. The wind and waves kept getting bigger. The spray from a wave crashing against the end of the ship reached her atop the wheelhouse. Waves rolling along the side of the ship reached the height of the deck.

Shortly after 7 p.m., Bell nearly died of fright as a huge wave washed over the *Fitzgerald* from behind, causing the ship to lurch. The wave completely covered the ship, washing along the deck and driving the bow down. It seemed a long time before the bow rose again. But a second monster wave followed the first one. The wind tore away Bell's screams. This time, the bow did not come up. The stern lifted a little as the bow went down, giving Bell one last look at the angry waters and snow-filled sky before she, the captain and crew sank below the waves with the ship.

It was a long, cold drop—over 500 feet down—before the ship came to rest on the bottom. Bell and the ship sat there, silent in death. Bell could see, though, that there were two sections of wreckage. So deep, and so cold were the waters that no one searched for Bell or the wreck for many months. Bell began to wonder if she, like the bodies of the crew, would remain there forever.

Bell continued to sit in silence until May 20, 1976, when a strange underwater craft approached. Later, she learned that it was a special dive team. Back on November 14, 1975, a Navy plane's magnetic anomaly detector showed there might be metal on the bottom—possibly a ship—at that location. Bell wished she could ring to them, "We're all still here!" The dive team circled the ship, pausing at the place where the name was clearly readable, 535 feet down, a mere seventeen miles north-northwest of Whitefish Point in Canadian waters. Then, they left Bell alone again in the cold, dark, twilight of the bottom of Lake Superior. Bell gave up and went to sleep.

Bell wasn't sure what woke her many years later, Tuesday, July 4, 1995, but she saw shadows of several ships high above. Two submersibles similar to the ones she had seen years before approached her. Bell could see people inside them with camera equipment. A special underwater cutting torch touched her at her base, freeing her from the roof of the wheelhouse.

She was removed and raised to the surface with new technology. Sunlight blinded her for a few minutes after so long in the dark. Then, she saw a 245-foot Canadian Navy ship, and one of the largest tugs out of Sault Ste. Marie, Ontario, and an eighty-five-foot private vessel. On the decks of the private vessel stood the fathers, mothers, widows, sons, daughters and other family members of those twenty-nine lost men. She heard soothing words from all around as a wreath was laid on the water directly above the wreck of the *Edmund Fitzgerald*. Flower petals fluttered over the waves and floated on the water that clear-weather day.

Bell heard speeches about how the governments of the United States and Canada worked together to raise her. She learned that one of the men holding those underwater cameras, Emory Kristof, was from the *National Geographic*, and that he had also been part of finding the *Titanic*. She heard that Sony Corporation had loaned the use of its brand new, high-definition underwater TV camera to film everything. Just as important, Bell heard that the Sault Chippewa tribe had co-signed a loan of $250,000 to the Great Lakes Historical Shipwreck Society. They had listened to the voices of the families who only wanted closure to their grief.

Bell watched people lower a copy of her, engraved with the names of the captain and crew. It would stay there as a permanent grave marker, attached to her old place.

With quiet respect, Bell was carried aboard the *Cormorant* (the Canadian Navy ship) to Sault Ste. Marie, Ontario. After so many years of silence and darkness, she was embarrassed by her condition. The people who walked by respectfully over the next few days did not seem to mind her darkened, dirty color. She watched in awe as Dianne Cunningham, Ontario Minister of Inter-Governmental Affairs, presented her to the families of the lost crew in a ceremony called "Call to the Last Watch." Slowly, as in a religious service, Bell tolled thirty times: twenty-nine for the men of the *Edmund Fitzgerald* and one more for all sailors lost over history on the Great Lakes.

Later that July, Bell was moved to another place inside a building, where she was cleaned and restored by the Center for Maritime and Underwater Resource Management, part of Michigan State University. All shiny and new again, they took Bell to the Great Lakes Shipwreck Museum at Whitefish Point. There she still sits, where people view her and think about all those lost on the Great Lakes. She is most honored to be there.

People may visit Bell seasonally—May 1 through Oct .31, from 10 a.m. to 6 p.m., daily, 18335 N. Whitefish Point Rd., Paradise Michigan, 49768 or call: 800-635-1742 or 906-635-1742 or visit www.SuperiorTapestry.com/sites for more info.

Fig. 3-2: Whitefish Point Museum Signage

Chapter 4 – Fox River Flowing

Fig. 4-1: The Fox River near where M-28 flows through the town of Seney.

Fox River, quite different from St. Mary's, formed around the same time, after the last Ice Age, but she did not tumble in rapids and flowed much longer overall. Lady Fox begins at a spring in higher ground slightly southwest of Grand Marias. She meanders slowly south through the central Upper Peninsula, curving back and forth through vast wetlands and forests. At last, she flows through the town of Seney and on in a generally southern course, until she joins the Manistique River. The water continues to flow south and slightly west and at last empties into Lake Michigan, near the city of Manistique. Numerous other rivers and streams flow into both these rivers.

Lady Fox was born when the weight of thousands of feet of ice melted and the land rose up slightly. Melt water formed her bed and filled lakes and marshes for miles and miles and miles. For hundreds, even thousands, of years, the central part of Michigan's Upper Peninsula has been one long stretch of flat wetland without mineral resources. In modern times, Lady Fox has heard some people, driving along M-28, call the area mind-numbingly boring. Great forests grew wherever the land was slightly higher than the marshes. All of it formed a wonderful place for water birds and migratory birds and many other animals that like plenty of water, and either didn't mind the harsh winters or could fly away from them. Undisturbed, trees of all kinds grew to great heights and girths and were homes and food for many kinds of living beings. Lady Fox River flowed on, also undisturbed.

Where the thickest parts of virgin white pine lined Lady Fox, two-and-three-century-old trees grew 100 to 150 feet high. Sometimes, the lowest branches were sixty to eighty feet above the ground. So dense were these trees in some places that there was no undergrowth because sunlight could not reach the forest floor. These giants ranged four to eight feet in diameter. If a winter blizzard toppled an ancient tree, the fallen log fed the growth of new seedlings as it rotted into the soil. Native People had no trails through the thickest of these pine stands, because with no undergrowth, there was nothing for other animals to eat, so it was useless to hunt there. Still, there was plenty of wildlife where Lady Fox flowed through wetlands, meadows and hardwood forests.

Each spring, as the ice and snow melted, Lady Fox watched life return. She heard birds begin to sing as they built nests to raise their young; watched various ducks, geese, loons and others hatch their eggs and then saw the babies swim behind their parents. She smiled as mother black bears led their cubs to her shores to drink and catch fish and watched chipmunks, squirrels and other small mammals scurry about searching for food. Many kinds and sizes of fish swam in her. In the shallow pools, thousands of frogs and insects joined the birds in a grand chorus of joy that winter had finally ended.

Days grew longer and warmer until midsummer. Babies of all sorts grew up along Lady Fox's banks, often with biting, buzzing and flying insects bothering them. Parents trained their young to hunt, graze, fly, run or hide from danger. Otters played and beavers worked on their dams, and every creature sought out her banks and pools for cool drinks. Orchids and every shade and size of wild flower kept bees busy in rainbows of color. Since every creature must eat, the cycle of the sun's energy went from the plants to the herbivores (plant-eaters) and omnivores (everything-eaters) and then to carnivores (meat-eaters) and, at their end, plants and animals returned to the earth by means of fungi and mold, that never-ending cycle of life, death and rebirth.

As the days grew shorter and colder and leaves turned from green to gold, yellow, red, orange and brown, Lady Fox watched as every moving creature prepared for what was to come. They ate everything they could and stored fat to sleep for months or to build up energy to fly south. Other animals stored food wherever they could to eat during the winter. Crisp days led to colder ones; frost replaced dew on the now brown and golden grasses. Every living thing prepared; it was the evening of the year, and Lady Fox flowed slowly and eternally on.

Snow finally flurried to the ground. Shallow places in the water froze quickly, while moving water kept other areas open for animals that did not sleep. Little animals, like mice and chipmunks, built complicated tunnels under the snow to connect themselves to stores of food, safe from those who hunted them. Foxes, coyotes and wolves followed their tiny tracks or the larger tracks of deer and moose, for they, too, had to eat during the cold months. A different kind of beauty covered the land, the river and her banks. In the stands of white pine, the trees seemed to sleep. Lady Fox liked this time of the year, as she loved each season in its own way.

Native people and then French fur traders did come for a while, hunting beaver and other animals for fur, but they went away after a while. For Lady Fox, life went on with its peaceful rhythm of the seasons.

Until the lumber barons came.

When people arrived in the 1880s, they said that the timber they saw was enough to last many generations. Lady Fox heard it said that these forests along her banks "would supply the entire county with lumber forever."

Near her banks, Lady Fox watched as men cut logs small enough for them to handle, built crude huts with them, chinking the cracks between the logs with moss and mud from her banks. She saw them cut a few crude windows into the sides, put in chimneys and cover the roofs with tar paper. Several such buildings, some larger and some smaller, stood in groups at various points along her banks, an ugly pox on the land (in her opinion).

Then, these men set out to build dams at what they called "strategic points" along her course. These were not constructed to last. Fox felt that the beavers did a much better job and wondered why they were doing this, since they weren't going to live near them. When the ground froze and the snow fell, more men arrived in each of these camps. With huge broad axes and crosscut saws, these men, throughout the winter, felled the trees, piled them along Fox's banks, all up and down her course. They took water from her to build "roads" of ice. This made it easier for them to slide logs from areas farther from her banks and stack them with the others. Fox noticed that each log had a mark burned into it.

Lady Fox watched curiously throughout the first winter of logging to see how this new activity would play out. Spring breakup came. Her ice cracked apart, and she began to flood where low areas along her banks filled with melted snow. Then, she discovered why the men had built those flimsy dams. When a head of water built up behind a dam, and floating logs piled up as well, the men broke these dams. Water cascaded out of them and logs flowed freely down to the next dam.

Build up; break dam; loose logs; build up; break dam... all the way down her course, into the Manistique River and beyond, Fox knew not where all the logs went.

A town called Seney sprang up along a part of her banks—more or less at the center of all the logging camps—and two railroads went through it: one going east and west; the other, north and south. The town turned into a terribly noisy place in the spring, once all the logs had been floated down past where she flowed into the Manistique. That was when the number of people in the town suddenly doubled, filling its many saloons, boarding houses and places of "ill repute." Men who had worked hard all winter felling, dragging, piling and running the tree trunks downstream now spent their money freely on booze and women. However, Lady Fox did see a few men go straight home to their families. Fox didn't know what went on in those buildings; she only knew that the peace and quiet she fostered throughout the forest and wetlands was no more. And she didn't like it—at all!

Lady Fox also watched as some men failed to respect her on those log runs. They took terrible chances when logs tangled and would not flow downstream. She watched as men with small knife points on their boots held poles and pikes in their hands—poking here, prodding there—to find which log must be loosened so the whole pile would flow again. More than once each spring, the bravest—or the craziest—pried the key log free. With a rushing whoosh, logs burst from being held, and sometimes the men did not get out of the way quickly enough and drowned in her frigid waters or were crushed between giant logs.

The other men dragged out their bodies and, because they were too far from town to take the bodies back, they buried these men in hastily dug holes, hanging the dead man's boots on the nearest small tree or bush to mark the place. Lady Fox thought that maybe if enough of these men died that way, they would all leave. But that didn't happen, not then, anyway. More came. She changed her attitude a little when she heard them talking. "Who will give a dollar of their pay to this man's wife and children?" the man who seemed to be in charge asked as one unlucky river driver was rolled into a hole.

Every man shouted that he would give. Fox felt somewhat encouraged by this show of generosity. She did have to admire the toughness of these men, but that did not make up for the fields of tree stumps—four to ten feet tall, depending on the height of the winter snow in a particular winter. This small bit of goodness she observed also didn't make up for the strange animals running wild along her banks—hogs and chickens that the people raised for food. They were not like the animals of the fields and less dense forests, which had begun to disappear as more people came. These new animals rooted up the dirt along her banks, driving away the playful otters and other creatures she loved. The pigs bred as quickly as rabbits, but there seemed to be no hunters (other than the people who let them run about) to keep their numbers in check.

The occasional generosity Lady Fox observed also did not make up for something else she saw from time to time. In the dead of night, a few men would sneak down to where logs floated along her shore, some of which were easy to reach. The men would pull out the end of a log, cut off the part where a lumber company's mark was and rebrand the log with another company's mark. She did not understand what they did, but anything done in secret in the dead of night was not likely to be good.

One winter, the East Branch of Lady Fox saw another interesting thing about people. The railroad between Seney and Grand Marais ran along that branch and crossed over her in one place. A great winter blizzard left nearly twelve feet of snow across the tracks. The train returning from Grand Marais to Seney became stuck in one such drift. A few people climbed out of the train and down her banks, filled buckets with water and returned to the train. Later, one man, wearing a pair of snowshoes, braved the storm and headed down the track toward Seney to get help, Lady Fox assumed. Though the snow was light and fluffy, the man struggled through it, and even with the snowshoes, it was exhausting and took him most of the night to reach the town. At dawn, two men with a dog sled headed back up the snow-covered tracks with boxes. Another train made its way up the tracks as well, clearing the snow ahead of it. Full of supplies, the sled reached the people stranded in the train, but it was two days later before the train finally completed its run to Seney. Lady Fox was impressed by how hard some people worked to help others.

Fox became more tolerant of these people, noisy as they were, during a week's break from cutting trees at Christmas and when all hell broke loose in the spring. She watched as Seney grew and grew until there were over twenty saloons, ten hotels, two large "bawdy" houses (and several smaller ones on back streets), two general stores, six drug stores, meat markets and even a jewelry store, along with one church. Once, two men walked along her shore during the summer, discussing how the town had gotten its name. One of the men said it was because there was once a Jewish fur buyer named Sheeney, then it got shortened to Seney. The other man insisted that was not true. The two of them argued on and on—neither one knowing for sure where the name had come from.

Fox also watched the day a man named Alger (who was one of the lumber company owners and running for governor of Michigan at the time) asked one of the river hogs, men who drove the logs down the river, how much he was paid. "We get $1.75 a day," the man replied.

"That's not enough," Alger stated. He ordered a raise for these men in their most dangerous work. However, subsequently, when the men went to collect their wages, they were only given the raise after the date on which Alger made the promise. Lady Fox heard much grumbling along her banks when they were told that if they wanted to continue to work, they must be rehired at the old rate. Some threatened a strike but then cooled off and accepted it.

"We could strike," Lady Fox heard one man say, "but there are many other men willing to work for lower pay. Lumber companies would just hire them and forget about us."

The lumber boom ended as suddenly as it began. Lumber barons took their money and moved on.

Those forests, that should have lasted generations, were gone in less than twenty years. Fox wept as she looked up from her banks. The tops of trees and the slashed branches littered the ground. Huge tree stumps stood out like bleached white grave stones in a cemetery all along her many miles of banks, and miles and miles back from each side. Her tributaries and what she could see of the Manistique River were similarly marred. People left in droves—some took the train north to Grand Marais, while others headed south, east or west—anywhere but Seney. Lightning strikes during spring and summer thunderstorms lit up the remains, a great cremation. Smoke hung in the air several days after each fire, stinging the eyes and choking any people or animals remaining. Lady Fox flowed through a war zone of destruction. Seney became a ghost town almost overnight. And because the forests were gone, most of the animals she loved were gone, too.

Fortunately, nature heals itself. Jack pines are the first to grow after a fire, and they sprung up quickly and groves of them grew taller each year, laying the way for other trees and grasses. With the free-roaming pigs and chickens gone, other animals returned to Lady Fox's banks. Speckled trout and other fish swam in her again. Seedling hardwoods sprang up here and there—the seeds blown by the wind or left in bird droppings. In only ten years or so, the land around Lady Fox began to look better, and she began to feel better. After all, she had watched the forests grow from nothing after the glaciers melted. It would take time, but it would happen.

People slowly returned, too, but for a different purpose. They came to rebuild their inner lives along her healing shores. One of them was a young man named Ernest Hemingway, who arrived for a vacation in September of 1919. He didn't talk to himself while fishing and remained mostly alone, but Lady Fox sensed his thoughts. Shortly before, he'd been part of a terrible war in Europe and his soul was troubled. Fox flowed past him, passing on her peace as best she could. Later, she heard that this man wrote a story, "The Big Two-Hearted River," based on his experiences fishing in her waters. His story was published in a collection of short stories, *In Our Time*.

Perhaps that story led others to the area to seek similar healing of their souls through nature. Over the years, more trees grew taller and taller—not like the great white pines had been, but they balanced new forests with areas of marsh and meadows, beautiful to the eye and wonderful for wildlife and birds.

Later, the United States Fish and Wild Life Service set aside thousands of acres, just east of Lady Fox, along the Dregs and Manistique Rivers, a place of rest and quiet for migrating birds, wildlife and people. Nature destroyed became nature renewed, a living image of the Phoenix. Come and visit; be renewed.

Seney National Wild Life Refuge, 1674 Refuge Entrance Rd., Seney, Michigan 49883

Open May 15 to October 20 each year. The headquarters' office is open 9 a.m. to 5 p.m., seven days a week all season. Ph: 906-586-9851

Seney Museum and Historic Depot, ph. 906-748-0831 or visit www.SuperiorTapestry.com/sites for more info.

Chapter 5 – One Piano's Plinking

Fig. 5-1: A Player Piano

This view of Piano shows clearly where the roll of music goes. The pedals are not visible near the base, since they are behind the bench.

Player Piano arrived at the train depot in Seney in the mid-1880s. He was anxious to see his new home, since he had gone directly from the piano factory, where he was built, to a train depot. While Piano had been moved a time or two from one train to another, with workmen complaining about his weight every time, he had not been anywhere but the baggage car of each train. Along the way, he had heard baggage handlers at various stations talk about the town where he was headed—it was reputed to be the "hell hole" of the world, the "toughest town" in Michigan's Upper Peninsula, where men out-cut, out-logged, out-fought and out-drank any other men in any known place.

Piano's first view, after the door of the baggage car rumbled open, was of a muddy street lined on each side with plank sidewalks connecting one business to the next. Piles of snow still stood half melted among the buildings. Piano could see rows and rows of small houses and a few larger ones behind the main street. Throngs of men, and a few "fancy" ladies, talked and shouted—some in laughter, some in anger. Two men in a fistfight barreled out of the nearest saloon and tumbled over each other into the mud of the street.

One man came running up to the baggage handlers. "Hey! That there's my piano. What will it cost me to have you haul it up to my saloon?"

"A full day's wages!"

"For two blocks?"

"You try moving this thing!"

"But its got wheels, ain't it?"

"Through that mud? You ought to be glad we ain't charging you three day's wages!"

So, Joe, the saloon owner, agreed to a day's wages. But before the baggage workers began, they decided it would be wise to lay planks along the street where the wheels would roll, so the whole thing didn't sink into the mud. While the baggage men laid down all the planks they could find, the saloonkeeper laid the thickest planks he had in his storage room to form a ramp from the door of his saloon to the timber sidewalk and down a step or two to the street.

Slowly but steadily, Piano made his way off the baggage car to the platform, and down a ramp to the planks laid on the street. When they got to the end of the planks, the saloon keeper picked up the ones behind and laid them ahead of Piano, and so the process continued. About two thirds of the way, one wheel on the back end slipped off the plank. Piano heard a long string of unrepeatable, unprintable words stream from the mouths of the baggage handlers. By this time, the whole procession had caused such a stir that half the town came out to watch.

A few hardy lumberjacks lifted the end of Piano back onto the planks in quick order, with promises of a free drink from Joe when Piano was safely inside his place of business. All told, it took a couple of hours, but to his great relief, Piano finally rolled in the door and rested against the wall of the saloon opposite the bar.

"What the hell you got that thing for?" yelled one of the lumberjacks sitting at the bar. "Nobody here knows how to play a piano!"

"That's the beauty of this player piano. You don't have to know how! You just pump the pedals and it plays itself," the saloon keeper boasted. "Here, I'll show you. Jake," he yelled at his employee currently serving drinks, "get these three jacks a drink; they lifted the thing up for me when one end rolled off the planks."

Joe then opened one of the boxes that had come with the piano, took out a roll, slid open a "door" in the front of Piano where music would usually sit and slid the ends of the roll into place. He placed a reinforced ring-hole at the top of the paper onto a small hook and cranked it to a starting position. The roll of paper was full of tiny holes and slits.

"Get that bench that came with it over here," Joe commanded. He sat on the bench and began to pump the pedals just above where Piano's regular pedals were. The pedals pumped air through bellows inside Piano. The tinny sound of a popular tune rose from him; the keys moving themselves, up and down according to the pattern of holes in the paper. Just like magic!

Everybody in the place clapped and stomped in time. When the song ended, the saloon keeper showed those around him how to rewind the roll to the beginning, put the song back in its box and load another tune. Boxes and boxes of tunes were carefully piled onto the top of Piano, their ends displaying the name of the song they contained.

"Hey, Joe," one of the best customers said, "how 'bout I give it a whirl?"

"Sure, Mack," the saloon keeper said. He proceeded to show his best customer how to use this wonderful instrument.

Mac looked at the titles on the boxes and chose one he knew the words to. Soon, the whole place was singing "Oh My Darling, Clementine" off key and on, tapping their feet, clapping hands and cheering loudly for more beer and whisky—which was exactly Joe's intention!

Joe's saloon quickly became one of the most popular in Seney. Some patrons pumped the pedals slowly, the songs groaning along. Others pumped much too fast, and everybody laughed as Piano's keys went crazy. Finally, everybody who tried it could hit just the right speed, although there were days and nights when the booze flowed too quickly and so did Piano's keys.

Over the years, Piano learned that there were times when the town and Joe's saloon were so crowded and noisy that he could barely stand it. The noisiest times came the week before Christmas (when the lumber camps let the men go home for a week) and just after spring break-up, when logging was complete for the season. Piano also noticed that many different languages came from the mouths of the men.

Often in the spring, a lumberjack would walk up to Joe and say, "Need you to keep my pay for me; dole it out just a little at a time, would you? Got to have some for later, 'cause last season, I drank it all up the first week. Went kind of hungry after that and the boarding house threw me out—no more credit."

"Sure," Joe said. "Do you need some now to pay this summer's room and board?"

"Nah, I done paid that up right away this year."

Joe nodded and took out a piece of blank paper. He wrote the man's name on it and the amount of money. "Each time I give you some, I'll write it on this paper." He handed the man a dollar to start.

The man nodded. A few hours later, that dollar was back in the barkeep's till. Piano watched several men moan and groan, begging for one more drink after they had spent all their money, firmly resolving to mend their wild ways. Some of those resolutions were kept, others lasted only a day or two.

There were other days in the spring when the yelling and fighting got so bad that Piano couldn't hear his own keys plinking. On more than one occasion, a head or two got banged against the keys or the person pumping the pedals. Sometimes, it seemed the men were just looking for a fight, or two rival camps would put their best men up against each other in a no-holes-barred, two-fisted, foot-stomping, dig-their-hobnailed-boots-into-each-other's-faces brawl. The local doctor had a lot of men to patch up every spring. Afterward, the rivals often acted like nothing had happened—best friends again. In spite of their roughness, Piano saw that the men did live by a code—of sorts. Even the bawdy ladies plying their trade received a certain level or respect. Tough guys often trounced a bully who preyed on the weaker men.

Piano liked the quieter times after most jacks had spent their winter earnings, $25 to $30 a month for four months, with the river hogs getting a little more. It was especially quiet after Christmas until spring break-up, because if a worker left the lumber camps before the season ended, Piano heard, he did not get paid. He also heard that no liquor was allowed in the camps, which explained why the men were so rowdy when the season ended.

Piano rather enjoyed election years. The various candidates, and even some at the state level, visited Seney trying to get votes, which often involved buying drinks for everyone in the house. Political argument often rose in volume, but remained civilized—for the most part. While the men enjoyed free drinks, they listened to the politician talk about what he would do for them if elected. A little while later, that politician's opponent would come into Joe's place and there would be more free drinks and another speech. Piano watched Joe smile and pocket all that drink money every election season.

During the quieter times, Piano learned much from the long nights of storytelling and the conversation of the saloon's patrons. Imaginations swelled with the warmth of the burning logs in the potbellied heating stove. Some stories grew bigger and bigger with each telling.

One quiet afternoon, Piano heard a curious conversation between Joe and one of the lumber company owners.

"I can't figure out why we seem to be short so many logs when they are counted out in Manistique," said the owner.

"Didn't know you was losing any," replied Joe.

"Well, I expect to lose some. A few logs float off in the snow melt flood or get hung up on a sand bar when the water drops, but the last two years, I lost way more than that."

"Any idea what's going on?"

"I've got my suspicions, but I can't prove anything," the owner said. "Going to try something tonight. I'll let you know if it works."

At that point in the spring, the logs had all floated south beyond Seney and into the Manistique River. The lumber company's owner was gone a couple of days, but when he came back—on another quiet afternoon—he told Joe what he'd learned. Piano tuned into their conversation again.

"I need a stiff one, Joe, to figure out how to solve this," the man said.

Joe poured him a shot of whiskey and set the bottle down next to the glass, waiting to hear what had happened.

"I slipped down along the river the last two nights, quite a way south. Good thing it was clear and the moon full, or I'd have tripped more times than I did. But it was worth it. I got to this one place where the banks of the river make it easy to get in and out. Heard some noise and went quietly to see what it was." He downed his whisky, and Joe poured him another.

"Bunch of thieves pulled out several of my logs, cut off the end with my mark and remarked them!"

Joe thumped his fist on the bar. "Damn thievery! Sounds like the cow pokes out west rustling cattle. Recognize any of them?"

"No, too dark for that and would be even harder to prove in court. Guess I could hire more river hogs to stay close to the drive, even at night, but then I'd barely break even."

The two men stared at each other. Joe poured himself a shot and stared at the owner, who was also a friend.

Finally, the owner said, "I wonder... the railroad is already halfway to Grand Marais... what if I sent my logs north by rail, skipping the river from here to Manistique?"

Over that spring, summer and fall, the owner was busy making necessary "arrangements" to get the railroad completed and begin building a lumber mill in Grand Marais. Piano was not able to get all the information he would have liked to hear, since that particular owner did not come back to Joe's much after that. Piano didn't often remember names, but he was quite sure he heard the Alger-Smith Company named as the one involved with investigating log theft.

Not long after, lumbering died out in that area, as well as the town of Seney, along with Joe's saloon, and Piano—with all his rolls of music—with was pushed out of the bar, down a ramp, along a hot dusty summer street (without the planks used to take him to Joe's place) and onto the train north to Grand Marais. There, Piano was pushed and pulled into one of Grand Marais' saloons. He wasn't the only one to move to Grand Marais. Some houses and buildings in Seney were taken apart, loaded onto flat cars and rebuilt in Grand Marais. That town's population grew from a few hundred to several thousand almost overnight, enjoying a boom of its own.

Piano enjoyed Grand Marais. It did get lively in the spring, but overall, it was more peaceful on its worst days than Seney had been on its best days. The lumber companies there cut the timber by hand; the train came and left regularly bringing in new people and not just lumberjacks. Sawmills cut the logs into boards, shipping out finished product. Sidings on the railroad reached farther into the forests so more timber could be cut without depending on which way streams flowed, and they could be cut that way year-round. A sawdust burner was built to use that waste material to power the steam engines that ran the saws. Piano heard that the sawdust burner even produced a small amount of electricity for some hours on some days. Men could have a steady income all year, and they settled down to raise families. A veneer mill, a shingle mill and other lumber related industries also provided jobs. Fishing boats plied the waters of Lake Superior for local consumption and also shipped loads of fish east and south.

Piano heard people rejoice in 1895 when the town built a new high school and then constructed a public water system. A new century arrived. The number of stores and businesses steadily increased. In 1906, the owner of the saloon, where people pumped Piano's player pedals and sang along to his tunes, put in a new-fangled thing called a telephone. The saloon owner could talk to other business owners all over town with it or call a constable if someone got too rowdy. *Ah, yes, this is the life for me,* Piano thought. When the bar was closed on Sundays, he enjoyed the music and singing coming from several churches. Those songs were quite different from the ones played on him.

Piano heard people discussing how busy the harbor was, and how dangerous the coast between Whitefish Point and Grand Marais—all the way along to Munising—could be. More than once, Piano heard it called the "Graveyard Coast." On long winter evenings, people told tales of many shipwrecks and were glad when the Army Corp of Engineers built a series of lighthouses and lifesaving stations at Grand Marais and to the east. Many times, those lifesaving people came in to celebrate after they had braved a storm to reach a ship in trouble and had saved many lives.

Piano heard the talk when more people came to town to deepen the harbor, because shipping continued to increase. The harbor area had been naturally divided into east and west bays, but a sunken ship blocked one part. They dug a new channel and built several docks along the shore. All this supported the barkeep and kept Piano's keys plinking merrily without all the many brawls he'd experienced in Seney. Piano listened eagerly to the stories he heard. He became aware that there were families who never entered the bars and did all their socializing with their church groups. But there were always the "regulars" who came in every night to tell stories, listen to Piano and sing along with his songs.

In 1908, Piano heard that the Manistique Railway, which ran from Manistique through Seney to Grand Marais, had taken thousands of people back and forth. Most of them were visiting relatives or had business interests in the town or beyond, but some came to live there.

Then the proverbial other shoe dropped.

The following year, a recession hit the whole nation and reduced lumberjacks' pay a lot and that quickly affected everything else. A greater shock came when the Alger-Smith Company decided to abandon the entire railroad from Grand Marais to Curtis—over ninety miles, including smaller branches and sidelines that had hauled logs to the mainline. Appeals to various federal agencies to keep the town's life-line open fell on deaf ears. A bit of hope came when the Manistique Lumbering Company bought the railway. But shortly after that, the company announced it would no longer run the railroad!

As the lumber companies left, the only good thing was a gift of land for a park donated to the township by one of the bigger lumber barons, Henry Gamble. It would be named Woodland Park.

Like rats leaving a sinking ship, many people packed up what they could carry and left town before the last train departed on November 5, 1910. Piano was left alone in the saloon—considered too heavy to attempt to take elsewhere. No one came and played him. Dust collected in the silence. Cobwebs grew from the corners into the entire place. He heard fewer and fewer church bells ring.

Seasons came and went in deadly silence. Piano sat in complete despair.

Then, eons later it seemed, Piano began to hear sounds from outside the sad building where he sat. A man named Otto Niemi unlocked the door and daylight fell on Piano. "Well, well, what have we here?" Otto asked. He brushed the dust off a bit of Piano and poked a key or two—plink, plink. "How about that! This would be great in our parlor."

With help from several friends, Otto rolled Piano out of his dungeon. Those helping Otto remarked about how he had dismantled an entire abandoned house, with permission of the absent owner, and rebuilt it on his own land. So much had been left behind when people deserted the town. Why not take things and put them back to good use? Otto collected a lot, and his son Axel picked up even more, with permission of absent owners who had abandoned the stuff in the first place.

Once settled in the parlor of the Niemi house, Piano learned that they were fishermen and their business had not only survived, but had grown a bit over the years. While they were far from rich, they got on just fine.

In 1919, the State of Michigan authorized the building of a highway, M-77, connecting Grand Marais to Seney along the route where the railroad had been. Once again, there was a good way to reach the town other than by ship. Piano heard the family talk about the highway and the fact that Woodland Park had survived and had been developed into a campground. People from other parts of the state and nation began to come to Grand Marais to relax in the summer months and enjoy its beauty.

Over the years, Axel collected more and more of Grand Marais' history from various abandoned buildings. Axel bought the house next to the one his father, Otto, had reconstructed in the 1950s, and began to use it as a museum, which he called the Gitche Gumee Museum. He moved Piano into it. Tourists would stop by to hear him talk about the town's boom days and muse over his collection. Life was good again for Piano.

One other disaster hit the family fishing business, though. When the Welland Ship Canal in Canada opened, allowing ships to bypass Niagara Falls, the sea lamprey came up with it. Piano heard Axel explain to his wife that sea lampreys are eels with sharp teeth in a round suction-cup mouth that latch onto trout and other fish, living on their blood until the fish dies. Then they let go and latch onto another fish. They spread through the rest of the Great Lakes preying on lake trout. Piano heard the fishing family talk about how the population of Lake Superior trout crashed between the early 1950s and 60s until all commercial fishing was forced to close for a number of years while scientists figured out how to control the lampreys so the trout could survive. Tough times were again upon the town.

Axel ran the camping park across the street as a way of earning a living. In the evenings, he put on little concerts in his home, playing handmade musical instruments. He also played Piano, but as a regular piano, because Piano's pedal pumps had broken down over the years. Not only were there very few people who even knew how to repair them, the cost was simply too much for the family to bear. People enjoyed Piano as a real piano just as much as they had before. He delighted in his evenings and liked being admired as part of the museum. All the objects the family collected over the years preserved the town's history and had many stories to tell.

At last, the museum came to Karen Brzys. You can visit Piano, and many other historical objects, at the Gitchi Gumee Agate and History Museum, E21739 Brazel St., Grand Marais, Michigan 49839. Phone: 906-494-3000 during operational hours from Sunday of Memorial Day weekend through the end of September each year (or 906-494-2590 for the office/art studio).

Also visit: www.Agatelady.com or Karen@agatelady.com to get her book, *Superior Land and the Story of Grand Marais MI.* Visit www.SuperiorTapestry.com/sites for more info.

Chapter 6 – Portrait of Pictured Rocks

God's Picnic

Iron tinted peanut butter and manganese jelly
Oozing out of top pre-Cambrian white and bottom Jacobsville
dark sandstone bread
Topped with broccoli stalk trees
Refreshed with misty haze and icy soda spray of Lake Superior
These cliffs show us billions of years of formation and erosion

(Poem jotted down by the author while viewing Pictured Rocks in July 2019. It echoes her first thoughts of the area at age thirteen while sailing along those cliffs on her parents' thirty-three foot sloop, *Lorelei*.)

Cliff stands over 100 miles from the "other end" of the Jacobsville sandstone formation, He towers 200 feet above the south shore of Lake Superior and stretches for many miles between Munising and the Grand Sable Dunes near Grand Marais. Born of the same process as the twin brother he is joined to, and attached somewhere deep beneath Lake Superior, Cliff looks out over the water. Carved over and over by glaciers, he thinks back over what many people have said about him in the years since people began to travel along this shore.

The Ojibwa called him *Nauitouchsinagoit*, (red likeness of the devil) and left him offerings of tobacco when they paddled by. They knew how treacherous the lake could be, and when passing Cliff, they had to paddle many miles with no place to go ashore safely should a storm suddenly come upon them. Parts of Cliff had broken off many times when wind and waves pounded him and because of

Fig. 6-1: Pictured Rocks National Lakeshore

the ice every winter. Over many years, these rocks at his base slowly became sand again. Carved along his length, people imagined the shapes of castles, battleships, arches, profiles and caves. He always accepted the ooohs and ahs with humility.

"Nature has made it pleasant to the eye, the spirit and the belly," said Pierre Espirit Radison, the first White person known to pass by him, riding in an Ojibwa canoe in 1658. But Radison was less interested in beauty and more bent on getting past that treacherous stretch of shore. He wanted to reach places where he could trade his goods for furs to take east and south—furs that would earn him hard cash much more valuable than the goods he gave to the Ojibwa.

Many years later, Henry Schoolcraft wrote of Cliff:

> "All that we have read of natural physiognomy of Hebrides, of Staffa, the Dore Holm, and the romantic isles of the Sicilian coast, is forcibly recalled on viewing this scene, and I may be doubted whether in the whole range of American scenery, there is to be found such an interesting assemblage of grand, picturesque and pleasing objects."

Henry Schoolcraft lived among the Ojibwa quite a while, learning their language and legends, completing a book on Ojibwa culture.

Another famous writer, who never visited Pictured Rocks, Henry Wadsworth Longfellow, had read Schoolcraft's work. He wrote down an Ojibwa tale of how Hiawatha encountered his enemy, Pao-Pak-Keewis, and destroyed him on these rocks. Cliff wondered who would win the clash of ideas he observed: romantic beauty and science or economic development. While he enjoyed the compliments on his looks, Cliff sometimes wished people would simply leave him alone.

Winter ice continued to creep into his cracks and, gradually, winter after winter, made those cracks wider until one storm or wave would be the final one, sending tons of him crashing down into the water. Cliff had no control over this process of erosion but he was pleased that this happened often enough to keep people from spending too much time around him. So, economic development of other areas of the Upper Peninsula won that particular round. Cliff may have smiled as erosion continued. There was plenty more of him behind each piece that broke off.

In 1850, a group of men built a "resort" they hoped would attract genteel travelers who loved beautiful places. But the only way to see Cliff was to travel by ship to Grand Marais or Munising and then take a smaller vessel for a close-up view. He heard the complaints of the few who did come. It was too difficult a journey—no railroad. They were used to traveling in luxury. These conditions were much too primitive. Where were the good wines and fine china? The few who did make the effort pleased Cliff with their words of praise, but the "resort" did not last even one year.

Cliff noticed a steady increase in the number of ships passing by him. He couldn't see what they were loaded with, of course, but the number of people increased, which resulted in more ships foundering along that shore. Cliff watched as people built the Au Sable Lighthouse in 1874. Its powerful beacon could be seen seventeen miles out into the lake, warning ships to stay far away from Cliff and other dangers. He also watched as people built a huge "slide" on the dunes at his Grand Marais end, down which glided huge logs, the trunks of trees cut south of him. These were rafted together along the shore and then loaded onto ships at Grand Marais. If they were cutting trees south of him, Cliff reasoned, they probably cut the trees elsewhere. So that was one thing people carried on—at least some of those ships passing by.

Once the railroad reached Seney, then Grand Marais and Munising, Cliff noticed another change. Small excursion boats began to leave Munising to cruise along his base shortly after the beginning of the 20th century. From the conversation of the people on these ships, Cliff learned that there were great mineral resources deep underground not too far from him: huge iron ranges to the west and southwest of him and unimaginable amounts of copper not far from his twin brother. Ahh, that was what had brought so many people and steamers! But there were still only few people with leisure time to do pleasure trips.

During the 1920s, Cliff heard that the Hotel Williams had been built in Munising, once again to try to attract people of wealth to visit the area. While this hotel managed to stay in business, its fame, and that of Cliff as a place to visit on vacation, spread very slowly. The decade of the 1930s brought everything to a halt in what Cliff heard called the Great Depression. Nobody had any money to do anything for a long time. Cliff didn't mind that a bit.

It really wasn't until after people had used up most of the timber and copper, and a great deal of the iron, that anybody began to think about the Upper Peninsula's great natural beauty as something to bring visitors. Even then, it took another twenty years for Cliff to see any sort of tourist boom. But those who came during the late spring, summer and early fall rode by on double-decker excursion ships. These ships stayed a fair distance from Cliff's sometimes dangerous base line, but many smaller private boats began to come quite close to shore, some even pulling up on one small beach about half way along his length. Then people built a road that came part way along his top. It narrowed into a path that many hiked or biked for miles.

People in Munising rejoiced On Oct. 15, 1966, when President Lyndon B. Johnson signed Public Law 89-668, creating Pictured Rocks National Lake Shore. Cliff couldn't help but hear about it. He and much of the land behind him, along with the dune areas around Au Sable nearly to Grand Marais would be protected. Since that day, Cliff has heard several people say that there was now a concept of balance between saving nature for recreation and economic development. At last, Cliff would be properly revered, but still left alone. There would be more development, but not too much, so that generations yet to come would be able to see how truly remarkable he was, is and will continue to be.

Cliff now watches in silence as people "oooh" and "ahhh," going by him in those excursion vessels, small private boats, kayaks and canoes, or hiking and biking with backpacks along his crest. People swam, fished and hunted near him. A smaller number took a bigger risk to see spectacular ice caves that formed along the shore every winter. Then, they skied or snowshoed along his rim, or used snowmobiles, that Cliff considered noisy, to view his winter splendor.

Of course, there are always those who did not respect Cliff, or forgot that he was continually eroding, or taking Lake Superior's gentle summer mood for granted when they shouldn't. Cliff witnessed several kayaks capsize in 2012 and a person drowned near Miner's Beach. A man fell to his death at Miner's Falls in 2013. Part of Grand Sable Dunes closed in 2014 due to high lake levels eroding away a huge portion. The Log Slide Overlook had to close in 2017 for similar reasons. In the summer of 2019, a large portion of Cliff collapsed into Lake Superior, very close to about fifty kayakers. Cliff was glad that no one was injured that time. Thanks to modern technology, a few cell phone videos captured the avalanche.

Cliff will never call out to you; you must seek him. Remember to honor him: "Take only pictures; leave only footprints." There is no need to leave gifts of tobacco, as the Ojibwa did.

Pictured Rocks National Lakeshore office Ph.: 906-387-3700 weekdays year round. Visit www.SuperiorTapestry.com/sites to watch a video relay of a cliffs collapse and learn more about Pictured Rocks.

Chapter 7 – A Plum Assignment: Sand Point Lighthouse

Fig. 7-1: Sand Point Lighthouse

It's easy to see why Sand Point Lighthouse was considered such an assignment by its keepers, and why they did not leave voluntarily.

Lighthouses instinctively know that sailors depend on them to send out a warning of dangerous waters. They are built to pierce the darkness and show where safety lies; blare out their locations with a fog horn or bell that can be heard for miles. Many a ship had been lost on the Great Lakes for the lack of a lighthouse, and many have been saved by those wonderful beacons and blaring horns. If towns were to be built to take advantage of the vast mineral and forest resources across the Upper Peninsula, supplies had to come by ship. Schooners, steamers and whalebacks came into Little Bay de Noc and Escanaba on a regular basis, carrying loads of life's necessities in and tons of iron ore and lumber out. Sand Point Lighthouse knew she was important because boats of all sizes had run aground on the shallows of the bay.

The National Lighthouse Service authorized her construction in 1867. She was nothing fancy, just your "standard" one-and-a-half story rectangular brick building attached to a brick tower, on top of which sat a cast iron lantern room with a 4th order Fresnel lens. Total cost: $11,000.

Once her fixed red signal turned on, she took her job seriously. Her first keeper's name was John Terry, a man who said Sand Point was a "plum assignment" because the lighthouse was located on the shore, with easy access to town. He and his wife, Mary, would not be isolated for months at a time on some island where "cabin fever" could easily send someone over the edge of a cliff into a cold water death. They discussed such things frequently within Sand Point's walls.

Sand Point appreciated the fact that John was responsible in carrying out his duties, beginning in December of 1867. He often talked gently to her as he cleaned that Fresnel lens. "What a fantastic inventor that Frenchman Jean Fresnel must have been to come up with a design for a light that would shine miles farther than ever before! They say he's saved a million ships all over the world."

However, as John moved around the six-foot wide lens, cleaning its many angled sections, polishing, and wiping away dust and grime, he also complained. "You sure are a bugger to clean, though, with all these little slanted lens pieces. But I can't have dirt and grime dimming your light, even if it takes so much time to move all around, up and down, twelve feet every day!" John didn't understand all of the physics Fresnel had used when designing his lens but knew that capturing more light through sections of circles inside circles made the light shine farther. Everything about the light and lens had to be cleaned and checked daily, which took a lot of time. But that was the job John signed on for, and Sand Point appreciated his attentiveness.

John's wife kept their living quarters neat and tidy. They were a great team for four months, and then Mary had to cope with John's sudden death in April of 1868.

Sand Point wanted to cry with her, but Mary soldiered on, keeping up both the inside of the house and the light tower. She simply did what had to be done, becoming one of the first women to be named a lighthouse keeper. She cooked her meals, kept her house, went to town for supplies and kept the lens and light clean and bright for a many years. Sand Point tried to cheer her on by shining extra brightly out over the shallows, which it was her job to do, and blaring out her warning when fog rolled over the bay. She was proud of Mary.

"Don't come too close!" the light and horn bellowed. "If you do, you'll run aground on that sand." From her high vantage point at the top of the tower, Sand Point enjoyed watching the fruits of her work, as ships of many sizes moved safely in and out of the harbor. On the docks, workers labored to unload food and supplies of all sorts that the people of the area needed. It was especially busy in the fall, when everyone stocked up on everything they needed to get through the long winter ahead. If ships in late autumn failed to arrive for any reason, people would go hungry, or worse. The light also liked to watch as the ships were reloaded with iron ore from mines to the north and west or huge trunks of trees or cut lumber from the miles and miles of forests all around.

Mary remained Sand Point's official lighthouse keeper many years, and she also talked to the lens and light. Lighthouse and light keeper were as one, a team, always on the lookout and responsible for their duties. However, Mary did leave during the winter months when there was no shipping. Sand Point stood tall but lonely and looked forward to spring and Mary's return. "Did you miss me?" Mary asked every spring. "All winter I've been earning a bit extra as a housekeeper for a family. I'll get you all polished up. Shipping will begin again soon. The ice is almost off the bay." Sand Point liked the years when she needed maintenance, and workers arrived in the winter months to fix her walls and roof.

Then, one day in March 1886, a fire broke out in the house, and Mary could not get out in time. Sand Point feared that she would be destroyed, but the tower remained undamaged. Sorrowful people from the town removed Mary's body, burying her next to her husband.

Lewis A. Rose was immediately appointed "acting keeper"—even while Sand Point was still under repair from the fire. The light had to continue to shine every night! Lewis Rose was acting keeper for three years before being officially named the keeper of Sand Point Lighthouse. He continued to attend to her, her lens, cleaning and fueling, all the way to 1913. As she had with John and Mary, Sand Point grew to feel quite attached to him. But people do not live as long as bricks, and Lewis reached the point when his body failed him. He could no longer climb the stairs in Sand Point's tower and was forced to give up light keeping.

The years marched on and on. Sand Point was repainted from time to time, repaired when necessary, kept up by light keepers and their wives. Sometimes, Sand Point was delighted to see babies arrive, play and grow up. She kept shining continuously under the National Light House Service until 1939, when the Coast Guard took over managing all navigational lights.

Shorelines never stay the same, always changing their shape as waves, storms and ice erode them. Currents move sand around; streams and rivers deposit silt when they enter a lake, sometimes creating deltas. During all those years, Sand Point watched as the channel and harbor at Escanaba were dredged deeper, from time to time, so larger ships could enter, or when silt and shifting sand began to fill the channel. The dredged-up mud was dumped on the shore, forming more land between Lighthouse and the sand bar she warned mariners to avoid. She found herself farther and farther from the shore and this concerned her. How could she continue to do her job properly when she was so far from the water? She watched with mixed feelings as people built a "crib" light several hundred feet from the shore. They dumped rocks and other firm materials into a crib of beams pounded deep into the bottom of the bay and other beams, which formed walls above the water to make an artificial island. On one hand, Sand Point was glad that any structure would continue to warn ships of the dangers of the shallows. One the other hand, she wondered, *What will become of me?*

Sand Point needn't have worried. She became the family residence of the Coast Guard Officer-in-Charge. The Coast Guard made several major changes. Her lens and lantern house were removed.

That took ten feet off the tower and the circular stairway. People built stairs inside and expanded the upstairs to include a bathroom and three bedrooms, with windows cut into the original walls. Sand Point rather liked her "makeover," but she was saddened that she no longer had the job of shining out over the water. Some years later, there were more alterations to her design—sheet insulation and aluminum siding.

Many happy years went by for Sand Point, while various Coast Guard officers lived in her for nearly two generations. It was a different, but still, satisfying life. But, once again, bricks last longer than people. In 1985, the Coast Guard decided to discontinue use of Sand Point. The crib light was automated and a lighthouse was no longer needed. Utter dejection rolled over Sand Point as she heard them plan to raze her.

"No, no, please not that," she yelled, though of course, no one could hear her.

Even though her plea was a silent one, someone understood and paid attention. The Delta County Historical Society took great interest in her, arranging to lease the building from the Coast Guard and raise money to restore her to the way she was originally. Oh, how lovely it was to hear the news that in the historical society's archives lay the original plans from 1867. All those changes to her since 1939 were stripped away. A duplicate cast iron lantern room came from Poverty Island with an authentic 4th order Fresnel lens. Sand Point was back to her enduring brick, one-and-a-half-story self with her tower exactly as it had first been built.

Sand Point stands proudly now as people walk through her, seven days a week and on holidays from Memorial Day to Labor Day, between 11 a.m. and 4 p.m., looking at what life was like in the past and learning about how important she was when first built. She is happy to know that a lens identical to her original is enshrined in the Delta County Historical Museum next door and pleased with the number of people who worked so many volunteer hours to keep her alive. Sand Point would be happy to see you, too, at: 16 Beaumier Way, Escanaba, Michigan 49829. Phone 906-789-6790 and also arch@deltahistorical.org. Visit www.SuperiorTapestry.com/sites for more info.

Fig. 7-2: Sand Point Lighthouse – Fresnel Lens

The red light inside this replica of the lens in the Sand Point Lighthouse may not seem strong from within the glass case and in daylight, but mariners could see it's warning from many miles away.

Chapter 8 – Ring 'Round the Ages

Fig. 8-1: Rings engraved with "HIS"

Here, you see Ring and the others found with her. Their small size makes it impossible for archeologist Paquette to push them farther onto his fingers. Photo by Paquette and used with his permission.

Note on fact vs. fiction: While this chapter is based on research, no one can ever know exactly how the rings and beads, one of whom tells her story here, made their way from their makers in France to a remote site in Marquette County, MI. So, while the events in this chapter are probable and realistic, they may not have happened exactly this way.

Ring, made of brass and to fit a woman's finger, came to life as the craftsman carved the letters "IHS" into a flat, round area on the top of the ring. The letters meant "Jesus" to the Jesuits, who often wore larger such rings, but mainly carried them around in a pocket to give to other people as a symbol of faith. Ring was made in France somewhere around 1630—though she was never sure of the exact year. Once completed, she was tossed into a cloth bag with many other rings just like her, as well as others with hearts etched into them. These were meant to be given in friendship to anyone, even children. Ring heard the craftsman refer to her and the other rings as "iconographic" as he handed the bag of rings to someone with a male voice who came to pick them up.

Ring could no longer see what was going on around her, but she could hear sounds and muffled voices. Other bags of objects joined the bag of rings in a barrel. When more things were packed on top of her, Ring could hear even less of the sounds outside the bag, but the other objects relayed information down to the bottom of the barrel. There were bags and bags of colored beads (in various shapes, sizes and colors), iron needles, pairs of scissors, spools of thread and knives. Items at the top said that they saw bolts of cloth and other goods piled all around their barrel before the lid was hammered in place. Other barrels held axes and tools, and there were piles and piles of brass kettles suitable for hanging over an open fire. It seemed that they were all in the hold of a sailing ship and the talk from the bolts of cloth was that they were headed on a long sailing journey across the Atlantic Ocean to New France. No one in the hold quite knew where, or what, that place was, but it seemed as though it would be quite an adventure. The word "trade" had been spoken frequently.

A few days later, everything in the ship's hold could hear shouts and commands above them. "Weigh anchor! Hoist main sail!" and a string of other orders. They felt the ship begin to move, slowly at first. Then there was a shift as the ship leaned slightly to one side and began to move faster. Ring could hear sloshing of what she assumed was water rushing along the sides of the ship, since her barrel was near the ship's hull and her bag was on that side of the barrel. Some of the bolts of cloth could see a bit of sky through an open hatch and said that several huge white sails billowed above and caught the wind, pushing the ship forward.

Gradually, the ship rocked all the trade goods to sleep. Ring had no idea how much time—days, weeks?—passed, because she had yet no real idea of time or even much idea of what the world looked like.

At one point, everything woke up to roaring wind and shouts of alarm, as salt water and rain splashed down the hatch. The bolts of cloth said it was a terrible storm—all the sails were down and the men on deck seemed to work harder than ever as the ship pitched up and down, back and forth. Sailors continued yelling to each other, but their voices were lost in the wind to the things below the deck. Ring, and the others with her, felt fear for the first time in their lives. Ring hoped never to go through anything like that again. Finally, the storm passed, everything dried out and gentle waves rocked them back to sleep.

One sunny summer day, the bolts of cloth reported that the ship had reached New France. The ship sailed up a wide river for a few days and tied up to a crude dock in a place the sailors called Quebec. Everything was hauled up from the hold of the ship and placed in piles inside a fairly large building made of logs and crude planks. Its size was that of a small warehouse, reported the bolts of cloth. They had been in such a place before.

After a week or so, a whole flotilla of canoes pulled up on the shore. Strange men, women and children got out and began to talk to the men from the ship. Ring heard strange words, but a bearded man in a black robe interpreted between the two groups. The new arrivals carried in bales and bales of something. The bolts of cloth didn't know what they were, but words in French indicated piles of the furs of various animals: beaver, muskrat and ermine. Both men and women began to look at all the trade goods that had arrived on the ship. Each bag in a barrel was opened and placed on a long, narrow plank table so the people could look them over. Finally, Ring caught a glimpse of her new world. Even if she could have spoken, no one could have heard her, so overwhelming was the jumble of voices, the rank odor of stale sweat and the brightness outside the wide door of the place next to its dull interior.

Several women *oohed* and *ahhhhed* over the rings, beads, knives, scissors, needles, thread and brass kettles. One of the Frenchmen pointed out barrels of liquor. "Makes you feel good," he said to a young man who came in with these new people. But the young man pointed to his head, made a gesture that indicated discomfort to Ring, then shook his head.

Ring soon noticed that the women, and not the men, seemed to be in charge of what items were chosen. A nearby axe that had quickly understood the language of these people said that a man had told others about how his wife had eaten special mushrooms during the previous moon so the spirits would speak to her. She then had visions of what they should receive for their gift of furs. "You get some drink after other things we need," Axe reported of what she said.

Ring heard one of the Frenchmen, who had lived in Quebec for quite some time, say that he would soon marry a woman of this band of Native people. "A good thing. I become part of her clan and then her clan trades only with me."

Axe had more to say about it later. "The marriage benefits both groups. It will ensure safety and survival for the Frenchman, and the woman will be able to keep her ears open for news of the world of Frenchmen a great distance away, passing on this information to her clan."

Ring was sorry she was not part of the big pile of goods in that particular exchange of gifts. Both groups of people celebrated their friendship for several days. Ring, four other similar rings, a needle, a pair of broken scissors—it didn't seem to matter that they were broken—a knife, thread and two handfuls of beads ended up in an animal skin bag belonging to a distant cousin of the woman about to be married. Two bolts of cloth and a big brass kettle were also loaded into the same canoe. The family, and several other families in other canoes, shoved off the shore into the current of the river, paddling hard since they were now headed upstream.

Once again, Ring could not see anything, because she was inside the bag, but the kettle told her that the large group of canoes paddled far up the river, then twos and threes of canoes branched off onto other smaller rivers and streams. The canoe in which Ring and the goods with her passed another settlement and then headed northwest on another, larger river that would later be named the Ottawa. Several days up this river, Ring's canoe pulled up on a sandy shore on the inside of a bend that this clan called home. All during the journey, Ring concentrated on listening to the words of the People, and she soon understood them.

The rest of that summer and fall, Ring and the other things with her sat in a wigwam as the women left daily to gather wild rice and berries to be stored for winter. There was a small hole in the seam of the bag, and through it, Ring saw piles of maple sugar the women had made in the spring and sometimes gave out in small amounts to the children who ran off smiling. But mostly, they worked to store enough food for a long, cold winter. The men hunted animals for food, fur, skin, bones and other useful parts. Ring watched as the women processed what the men killed into dried meat and bones to be crushed later and cooked for the marrow and nutrients in them. Small bones were shaped into awls and other tools. Animal stomachs and bladders became bags for carrying water. Furs that the French liked piled up in a corner of the longhouse, while other hides were scraped and tanned to make leather. Ring learned that the People did not have to make quite so many bone tools, since they had begun to trade with the French for better made, longer lasting iron knives, axes and hoes. These people stayed mostly in one place, hunting, gathering and even planting maize and squash, so the tools made a huge difference in their lives.

That winter something truly terrible happened to the clan. A Frenchman stumbled into the camp very ill with a fever. The people took him in—it seemed he was a cousin of the man who had married the woman in Quebec. He lay on a pile of furs quite close to Ring. No matter what bark and herb teas the women prepared, or how their wise medicine man tried to help, the Frenchman died. Even worse, the fever spread to others in the longhouse. Soon, it ran rampant and most of the clan lay ill or dying. One woman who managed not to become ill said it was because a certain man of the clan had failed to give thanks to the spirit of a deer he had killed. "I am not sick because I offered prayer to the deer's sprit as I scraped the hide for tanning," she said as she tended Ring's owner until she died.

When the sickness was finally over, the woman and her two children were the only ones left alive. Spring came and the woman loaded as much as she could into a canoe and left the rest behind. Included in what she took was the bag with Ring and the beads and items with her. The surviving woman paddled her family farther up the river and then onto another river, returning to the place of her birth. Once she reached the place, she became known as a "two-spirit" woman, because she had needed to take on the role of a man. Ring heard her referred to as "Iron Woman" or "half sky."

Iron Woman received a lodge of her own from her aunt, and to that aunt, she gave the bag with Ring and the other items. Aunt of Iron Woman sewed the beads and rings into a pattern on the deerskin dress which her daughter would soon wear on her wedding day. This dress was carefully packed into a canoe when the families of their clan traveled to *Bahweting* for the summer festival—which was where her daughter's and many other weddings would take place. The canoes went up one river, everything was carried a distance, then down another river, until they reached the large bay and many islands along Lake Huron's north shore. From there, it was a short journey to *Bahweting*.

Ring was a little disappointed that she was not to be worn on the woman's finger, but she let that disappointment go when she heard the words of praise for her in the center of the pattern on the deerskin dress. Sewn in as the heart of the pattern, she was surrounded by the other four rings with the beads spreading out like rays of the sun, a special pattern on a special dress for a special day.

Ring, this time part of an Ojibwa family, watched them load up their canoe, portaged up *Gitchi Gumi Sipe* into the great *Gitchi Gumi*, paddling west along its southern shore to their encampment. Ring watched the woman work all that fall. When winter came, she watched as the woman pounded the bones of a moose and boiled them so the fat and marrow could feed her husband and the child growing inside her. Ring was fascinated to see her heat large round rocks in the cooking fire at one end of the lodge and then use pieces of fur to lift the hot rocks out of the fire. She placed them in various places along the walls near the lines of beds in the longhouse they shared with other families. The rocks heated the whole place.

That, and many other winters, passed with warm fires, stories, women cooking, men making snowshoes and leaving to hunt, babies crying and children playing in the small space. As winter turned to spring, women left the lodge to gather maple sap, which boiled constantly in one of those brass kettles until it was syrup and, occasionally, until all the water was gone and the remaining maple sugar went into birch bark baskets with lids to be doled out carefully over many months. Years passed, children grew, the rhythm of the seasons always dictated the work to be done and it was never-ending, except for those summer trade and festival trips. Ring watched it all from the front of the woman's dress.

Then, one spring, the woman on whose dress Ring had been so many years, used a pair of broken scissors to cut all the beads and rings off her dress. The beads she sewed into a new pattern, along with several porcupine quills, onto another dress, for her own daughter, who was about to be married. She placed the rings, at last, on her fingers—three on her ring finger, including Ring, and the other two on her baby finger. Before her daughter left with her new husband, the woman slipped all the rings off her fingers and put them in her daughter's hand, saying they might make good gifts for children and other women in her new husband's family.

This young woman put Ring onto her own finger, then slipped the others into a small cloth bag tied to the band on her waist. Ring's new home was several miles inland from *Gitchi Gumi's* shore, along a trail used by many Ojibwa. Ring remained on the young woman's finger, but the others did go to children in her new family. The children were delighted! Ring watched the children put on, take off, put on, take off, play with, put on... until each of the other rings dropped from their hands to be covered in the loose dirt and pine needles covering the floor of the longhouse. Ring watched the children search in vain, but all their sweeping of hands and digging in the hard-packed dirt only sent the other rings farther down. Ring was glad she was on the woman's hand and had not become a child's plaything to lose during long winter nights.

The young woman's first daughter grew from babe, to toddler, to a little girl who constantly touched Ring with awe. Finally, one winter, "Here, it's yours," her mother said, "now be careful, don't lose it." About the same time, having obtained a new dress for herself, she folded the dress with the beaded pattern into a bundle and stashed it in a corner of the lodge. Ring lasted an entire moon's cycle on the little girl's finger before she found herself surrounded by dirt and pine needles. Ring called out endlessly, but of course the child did not hear her.

Ring didn't know why, but the clan never returned to that winter camp. As many years went by, the rings and beads found they could hear each other's voices faintly, but talking was so much effort and there was nothing to talk about—all they did was sit in the dirt. The lodge poles rotted and fell into a heap of wood, which turned into wet sawdust and then dirt. Animals came and sniffed at the piles. A mother wolf used the space under the brush as a den one year. Then nothing at all. Ring went into an endless sleep.

Noises finally woke Ring. Much later, she would learn that over 300 years had gone by, and the rumbling and voices she heard were men building a road right through that old encampment, which was hidden from their eyes, so they could cut down the trees. What had been the lodge, where Ring was buried in the dirt, was on one side of the road, while the place where the women had cooked food lay on the other. Then the noises ceased. New trees grew and the road was less of a road. Ring lay in the silence again, wondering if she would ever be found.

But one day, a man named Paquette walked down that two-track road in 1996, carrying a metal detector. Ring woke up. She seemed to recognize the steps of family, so she called out to that metal detector, setting off its beeping noise. Ring felt someone scratching the loose earth and, behold, there was Ring! Amazed, the man picked Ring up, brushed off the dirt and took a good look at his amazing find. Now Ring did not know until later that Paquette was what had long been known as Metis, a mix of French-Canadian and Ojibwa blood. He had said, "*Boozhoo*," that day, and every other day he returned to the site. When he found Ring, he knew it was a gift from his ancestors, and so upon leaving, he placed an offering of tobacco on the ground in thanks, "*Miigwetch!*" He truly felt a spiritual connection to the people who had once dwelt there, and Ring was a part of this.

Paquette studied Ring for many months. In his self-talk, she discovered what had happened over the years she lay buried. He returned to the site many times with others for formal archeological digs in 1999 and 2000, finding moose and beaver bones, the broken scissors, a needle, the other four rings that the children could not find—but then those children did not have the modern equipment and screen-bottomed boxes to sift the soil. Ring heard Paquette tell others that the reason all the artifacts were so well preserved was due to the clay-like soil of that particular area (mixed with moose fat and the like that helped preserve things). The site where Ring had been found was named Goose Lake Outlet #3, seven miles inland from Lake Superior in Marquette Township, south of the City of Marquette, east of M-35 and south of county road 288. Even the beads were found when they used a smaller grade screen on a second sifting.

Ring had a special storage place with the other rings. She listened as her new owner spent hours and hours researching her and the beads, asking himself constantly, "How did these things end up there?" Then he spent more hours looking up other comparable sites, and the items found in them, to estimate an accurate age of the articles. Ring had a front row seat when Paquette spoke to groups and wrote papers about his research after that archeological discovery not far from his own back yard.

Ring is very happy to be back in the light. Paquette knew that the gifts his ancestors led him to were meant to be shared, so you can see her and many other artifacts at the Marquette Regional History Center, 145 W. Spring St., Marquette, Michigan 49855 ph. 906-226-3571. Please visit www.SuperiorTapestry.com for more information.

Chapter 9 – A Failure in Forging Iron

Fig. 9-1: Signage at Michigan Iron History Museum

This photo of an informational sign at the Michigan Iron History Museum in Negaunee shows what the forge site once looked like.

The ground and the rock formations around First Forge told him how iron came to be deposited in the Upper Peninsula. He was fascinated. A couple of billion years ago, before the volcanic activity that laid down copper deposits, and before the Jacobsville sandstone formations, there was an inland sea with carbon dioxide and methane (i.e., natural gas) in the air above. This sea covered all the area that would later become the Upper Peninsula. Many watery eruptions and sea vents laid down layers and layers of iron. Much later, plants evolved, and so oxygen became part of the atmosphere. Things were like this for a billion or so years; then, there was a

Fig. 9-2: Overlook at Michigan Iron History Museum

This view from the overlook behind the museum demonstrates how nature has reclaimed the area on the Carp River where First Forge once stood.

period of mountain building. The iron-rich deposits, under intense pressure and even more volcanic heat, folded and fractured and then were uplifted into a mountain range. Nothing in geology ever stays the same. Even while the mountains were rising, they were already being worn away. Add to that another billion or so years and four Ice Ages, and the mountains were reduced to areas that were quite flat, but still fairly high.

The rock around First Forge also told him that fossils over 1.7 billion years old had come out of the nearby Jackson Mine and later the Empire Iron Mine—possibly the oldest "megascopic" formations of life ever found (this means that you can see them without a microscope or even a magnifying glass). First Forge figured any rock old enough to have seen the process was a reliable source of information. He was awed by the age of the iron ore that would go through his firing process.

One nearby tree told him how the first White people came to the area. The Ojibwa Chief Marji-Gesick led a man named William

Austin Burt to a place where one could break chunks of iron ore from the surface. William Burt's compass went spinning around, trying to find north. A year later, the same Ojibwa guides led Philo Everett and some of his partners to the same area. Philo knew nothing about iron and was actually looking for copper, but he had the intelligence to hire someone who did. Thus, Abram Berry became the first president of the Jackson Mine. But another tree insisted that was not how it happened. He said the Ojibwa chief certainly knew about the iron, but that different people had led Philo Everett to the site. But the first tree continued to argue. Back and forth they went, each stating that they knew for sure. First Forge finally ignored them; it didn't matter to him who was first or who led them there. His job was to process that iron ore into a usable form.

Forge did know from his own experience that discovering the ore was much different from mining and transporting it. He also listened to the men from the mine and those who kept his fires burning. The mine was some twelve miles inland from the shore of Lake Superior. These early miners had to carry on their backs ore chipped from the outcroppings to the mouth of the Carp River, where it was loaded aboard a ship. The ship could sail only as far as Sault Ste. Marie, and then the ore had to be portaged around the rapids of St. Mary's River, loaded onto a different ship and sent much farther south to be processed. When chipping away at the surface was no longer practical, a crew of three—two to pound the drill bit with sledge hammers and one to turn it— drilled a hole/tube for explosives, which would blast and fracture the ore body. Then, it was carried out of ever-lengthening tunnels and placed in wagons driven over a horrid plank road. That plank road was the result of numerous complaints about the difficulty of wagon transport (and sleighs in the winter) on a muddy track through the wilderness. The trees laughed, and so did Forge, but they had to admire the people's dogged efforts to make a profit.

Maybe it would be easier to ship forged iron rather than ore, these men reasoned. That was how, in February of 1848, First Forge came into being, three miles from the Jackson Mine on the banks of the Carp River. The best skilled iron workers willing to come that far north had been hired to build Forge. He was constructed to be the best firebox, hot air blast design of his time. They built a dam across the river with a waterwheel and a blacksmith forge at the base, along with cabins for the workers. Heat for the forge was produced by charcoal, so an "oven" to produce that also had to be built. Forge was proud to be the very first built in the Lake Superior region. In mid-April of 1848, the first bloom, a semi-finished piece of steel rolled to reduce size, produced a bar of wrought iron. By the following November, ten tons of wrought iron had come out of Forge. A man, E.B. Ward, bought the iron and used it to produce the walking beam, or backbone, of the steamer *Ocean*. This success led Forge to believe he would be used for many years.

The men continued that winter, in spite of the harsh weather and the difficulty of transporting the wrought iron to the lake. However, Forge heard the bosses say that it took three hundred bushels of charcoal to produce one ton of iron. An acre of timber yielded enough charcoal for five tons of blooms—a two-day output. The timber closest to Forge went down quickly, including the trees in that argument about who-led-whom to the iron first. Since trees were also used for log houses, cooking and heat, men cut trees and hauled logs over longer and longer distances. Timber disappeared at an alarming rate.

While First Forge could produce a lot of wrought iron, the costs went up and up. Paying the miners, paying the forge workers and lumberjacks, paying those who hauled the product to Marquette and Lake Superior, paying the ships to transport it... The cost came to $200 per ton, and the market rate was $80 per ton. Forge heard the men in charge discussing that.

"So, basically, we are losing $120.00 per ton!"

Another man figured the cost of shipping the unprocessed ore. Mining cost about $.50 per ton and hauling it to Marquette cost $3 per ton, and there, the ore earned $8 per ton, not forged. Not a huge profit, but with enough volume...

But what about me? Forge wondered.

Jackson sold his interest in Forge to General Joe B. Curtis of Sharon Iron Co. in Sharon, Pennsylvania. This company made some improvements to Forge's design to improve efficiency. Forge produced wrought iron, from time to time, through 1852-53, but he was still not profitable. "I'm trying," Forge said over and over.

In 1854, a group of employees formed Clinton Iron Co. and tried again. But if the fire was a little too hot, or not hot enough, or the "bloomer" was not paying attention, or there was not enough ore, the air blast failed... Forge couldn't control any of that—it was up to the people working him. They even used some of the slag, the material left over, to construct a better dam, repairing the upper layers. Slag also went into some of the buildings—less wood cut down from forests farther and farther from the site.

The men sighed. Forge sighed in his own way and tried to see the situation in a better light—he had helped prove that mining iron in the area could be profitable. He also heard the talk about how much easier shipping would be with the opening of the canal and lock around the St. Mary's Rapids. Things were definitely looking better for the mine owners, miners, lumberjacks and others.

But Forge sat idle. He'd been beaten by rough terrain, harsh climate and a lack of skilled iron workers willing to put up with those conditions on what Forge's owners could afford to pay them. Weeds grew around him, then small trees, which grew into bigger trees. The dam weakened with each passing season and finally collapsed. The Carp River covered parts of him with twigs and branches. Silt washed over the remains every spring when snow melt raged down the Carp's course. Even his stack of fired brick finally fell over and crumbled. Anything of use or value had long since been hauled away. While the mines grew along with the communities around them, Forge feared he was forever forgotten.

But some people had not forgotten First Forge. In 1904, the place where his remains lay was made into a historical site. It is now the home of the Michigan Iron History Museum. From the museum's overlook, you can see where nature reclaimed the place where Forge once stood, proud and productive, and you can learn a lot more about him and the history of iron mining in the Ishpeming, Negaunee and Marquette area.

First Forge's legacy is that people can learn from failure.

The Michigan Iron History Museum: 73 Forge Rd., Negaunee, Michigan 49866 ph. 906-475-7857. For more information, please visit www.SuperiorTapestry.com/sites.

Fig. 9-3: The Iron History Museum (2020)

Chapter 10 – Saturday Sauna

Fig. 10-1: Sauna at the Hanka Homestead

Sauna grew as Herman Hanka laid down the first six tiers of logs. His awkward walk and trouble using one arm made work on her walls slow. He never paid attention to his sons, Nik and Jaluu, when they yelled at him from behind, only responding when they touched his back or shouted in front of him. Sauna wasn't surprised when the boys took over building her upper tiers. As their father had taught them, they peeled the bark off each log, hewed the sides from round to square, scribed and gouged the lower side so it sat on top of the log below, fitting as tightly as possible and notched the ends so they fit the log below and were ready for the log above.

Built from pine, spruce and cedar logs, Sauna was delighted as her walls rose over several days to form a building twelve by nine feet—a steam room with a sheltered outside overhang on the gable end. Rocks picked out of the fields sat atop her stove, which was held with scraps of steel. Because softer rocks can burst and pieces fly when hot rocks are hit by cold water, the boys were careful to choose only basalt and granite rocks. Rough-sawn planks, nailed to the bottom logs and resting on bare earth, formed the floor. Three more log planks, attached to the side walls, served as benches. Cedar logs were split and covered with three inches of soil to insulate the ceiling, while two rafter plate logs and a ridge pole stuck out six feet in the front, a porch to protect those going in and out from rain. Other hewed poles acted as rafters and held up a split pole roof covered with sheathing and hand-split cedar shingles. A boxed air vent with a sliding door allowed the smoke to exit the room through the ceiling. There was also an air vent in the east wall. The boys carved Herman Hanka's name into the door. Sauna's final touch consisted of racks made of narrow branches suspended on wires, upon which the family laid fish and strips of meat for smoking.

The chunks of rock on the stove told Sauna that back when glaciers covered Michigan's Upper Peninsula, the hill where she stood rose above the ice, a little island of bare ground. When the great ice melted, the hill stood between the Otter and Sturgeon Rivers, only three miles "as the crow flies" from Keweenaw Bay of Lake Superior. Rock said that the hill, the shores of Otter Lake and higher areas of the Sturgeon River flood plain appealed to immigrant families from Finland as good farm land. He heard them say that the climate and forests reminded them of home. One family explained that the Homestead Act of 1862 allowed a head of household to gain ownership of up to 160 acres by building a house on the land and farming it for a certain period of time. "Good way to get a better life," Rock remembered hearing. So, people began to settle in that area in the 1890s; some settled along Otter Lake's shores. Others created the town of Tapiola.

"I always watched the families build their sauna first," Rock said. "I saw that it gave them a place to live while they built a farmhouse. How come you weren't first building on top of this hill?"

Sauna felt the need to correct Rock's mispronunciation of her name. "It's Sa-oo-na, not Sa-na."

"Oh, sorry."

"I'm not sure why they built the house first. But I can tell you I'm a *savu sauna*, or smoke sauna. Besides my main purpose for bathing, they can smoke meat in me, and I provide a warm, clean place with readily available hot water for mothers giving birth to babies."

"Well, they've got you and a house now," Rock said. "Bet they use more of the woods to build a barn, then sheds. Those boys were well-taught by their father! One neighbor kept yelling at his son that he wouldn't have a proper Finnish education if he didn't learn how to hew a log."

When neighbors came to welcome the Hankas to the community, Sauna heard Mary, the oldest daughter, explain that her parents, Herman and Miina, with her and the next three children, arrived in the Copper Country in the 1880s. Herman worked in the mines at Calumet until an accident left him mostly deaf and without full use of one arm. Mary went on to say, "He took out a homestead in Misery Bay. Mama gave birth to my two youngest brothers there, but she was not happy at Misery Bay—too far from neighbors. Papa traded that homestead for a shotgun and moved us to Tapiola."

"How could he get a second homestead?" the neighbor asked. "According to the Homestead Act, a man can't take out a second one."

"I turned eighteen in 1896," Mary answered. "This homestead is registered in my name. Someday, I'll probably turn it over to one of my brothers. We took out two forties."

"You could have got four forties."

"I know, but Papa said we really didn't need that much."

The first Saturday that Sauna was used, Herman loaded birch and maple logs into the stove. Sauna knew they would heat the rocks until the room was good and hot. Herman and his sons entered first and stripped off all their clothes. They sat on the cedar benches and sweated away accumulated dirt and grime as the heat opened pores in their skin. Jallu dipped a ladle of water from a bucket and tossed it onto the hot rocks. A burst of steam rose. Herman dipped a small birch bough into the bucket and slapped his back, arms and legs with it. Nik grabbed a bar of soap and worked it over an extra dirty spot on one foot, then rinsed with another ladle of water. Once the three of them were dripping with sweat, they left Sauna and ran down to the stream where they threw icy water over themselves to cool down (in winter they would roll in the snow).

Upon returning to Sauna to dress, Jallu said, "Ah, good to have that all-over tingly feeling." The other men nodded as they left Sauna.

It was the women's turn. While they undressed, Miina said, "I remember when all you kids were small, and we all took our sauna together. Those years were short before you six turned or so. Then, you were too old to see your father naked." She laughed and so did Mary and Lydia.

When the women went to cool off in the stream, Sauna thought how lucky the Hankas were to have that cold, sweet spring water running right through their land. Sauna watched over the next six years as the Hankas cleared new acres of land, some for root vegetables, such as onions and potatoes, some for cow pastures, some to cut hay for the cows' winter feed. She watched as they built a milk house right over the stream with a hole in its floor, through which jugs of milk and butter could be lowered to stay cold. Every Saturday, Sauna heard the women talk about the chickens or making *viiliä*, cultured milk like yogurt, and *juustoa,* oven cheese. Sauna watched as Mary left some mornings to trade their milk products and eggs with their neighbors for flour or bacon that they did not cultivate on their farm.

Mary left the farm in 1899 and married Otto Malineimi. Sauna heard Miina say her daughter gave birth to a son, Arvo. Sauna wanted to cry because that baby was not born in her warm steam room, but Otto had a good job selling Singer sewing machines, so they lived away from the farm for a while. Still, Sauna enjoyed watching the younger Hanka children grow up and learn about the farm and Finnish culture. Mary returned to the farm when Arvo was about five. Otto's work as a traveling salesman kept him away from home a lot; Mary wanted to be closer to her family.

Sauna watched as Jallu, Lydia and Arvo headed off on the long walk to the schoolhouse at Otter Lake. She beamed with pride when families on the hill came to say they agreed to Nik's idea to name the place *Askel*, the Finnish word for "hill." The farming community was granted a post office in 1908. Sauna knew it was not a Finnish man's way to talk at length or express much emotion, so she learned more from observation than conversation.

The work was long, hard and constant on the Hanka Homestead, and Sauna was there to rid them of a week's worth of dirt every Saturday. They were never what one could call "rich," but they got by. The women kept the house, fed the livestock and chickens, washed, cooked, cleaned, sewed and a million other chores. The men hunted, fished, planted and harvested, cut wood all winter to dry and cure for the following year—hard wood like birch, maple, and oak for fuel; pine, spruce and cedar for building or repairing buildings. Sometimes, Nik left to work in the lumber camps to earn a bit extra in the winter. He was also the area's blacksmith—often not charging his neighbors for these services. Sauna often saw men come to say thank you to Nik, after he had helped them build a new sauna or other buildings for their farms.

What an event it was in 1913 when Miina took out a mortgage on the farm to purchase a Model-T Ford! Nik drove children, their faces beaming, to school in that car over the bumpy corduroy road, going through Arnheim Swamp in high gear. Many children dragged their broken bicycles to Nik. He always fixed them.

"Pa," Nik said one night in Sauna, "I think we should sell half the farm to buy a horse to work the rest of it better." Herman nodded and it was done. In 1915, Nik announced, "Pa, if I cut and prepare logs for telephone poles, we can get a free phone." Herman nodded and it was done. During World War I, Sauna saw Nik and Jallu leave to work as loggers along Keweenaw Bay. The logs they cut and hewed went into the copper mines—an essential business during the Great War.

Sauna could not have been prouder of her family, or happy to be such an essential part of their lives. Herman had made a small pond in the stream between Sauna and the house, and in it he tanned hides by soaking them for weeks in vats with a solution of elder willow bark. Sauna laughed on more than one occasion when Herman managed to hear about neighborhood children and their plans to steal his special Yellow Transparent apples that he gathered into barrels to sell for cash around the community. Herman would send those naughty children running in spite of his inability to hear well. In her later years, Miina smoked a pipe and was very hunched over, but she always had *viiliä*, bread and butter for any neighbor children who stopped by. There was always plenty of apple pie with *viiliä* for Herman, and her jams and jellies were the best around.

Mary was around less and less over the years, because she worked as a cook for men in the lumber camps. Sauna heard from neighbors that Mary really didn't like children and was known to be crabby in the camps. Sauna also heard that Mary was grouchy around the women whenever she went to help out after someone had a new baby, and that Herman was "cantankerous" in his deafness. It seemed Nik was the handiest around the farm—a true jack-of-all-trades. Lovely Lydia didn't trust men at all as she grew up and liked to gambol about the woods talking to the trees. Sometimes, Sauna heard her say she did not want children; they would interfere with her lifestyle. She was always at home with her mother, making bread or butter, sewing clothes for herself or the others.

Jallu, who lived longest on the farm, was not much of a farmer but worked hard. He trapped coyotes and bear, hunted deer with a carbide lamp, a practice called shining deer, made wooden rakes, helped people build saunas and the like, made seaworthy wooden boats, tools and knives. The years went by. Life, though hard, was good. It was discussed in short sentences every Saturday night in Sauna.

In spite of all Sauna's hopes and dreams that Hanka grandchildren would be born in her, Arvo remained the only grandchild. Sauna became extremely jealous whenever the women talked of some other family giving birth in their sauna. She wished she could grab the ladle and pour water on those hot rocks until the women fled from the heat to the stream.

Nothing lasts forever. People grow old, develop health problems, and where another generation of children does not follow, homesteads fall into ruin. Mary died in 1921, and Nik, plagued with bad teeth which ruined his health, followed her in 1923. Sauna knew that was the beginning of the end of the farm, especially when Jallu converted the milk separator into a blower for his blacksmith shop. Children in other families on the hill drifted off to work in factories in Detroit, not keeping up farming traditions. Neighbors could still "set their clocks" by Herman's consistent two-mile walks to the post office, but that ended when he died in 1933. Miina and Jallu hung on, making a living as best they could. Jallu stayed on after his mother died in 1941. They were such wonderful, plain folks. Sauna gave up her jealousies to remember the good times.

She'd like to share all that, and more, with you when you come to visit the Hanka Homestead, perfectly restored to its 1920 state. It's a bit of a drive to get there: you'll turn onto Arnheim Rd. off of US 41, a bit north of Baraga, and drive about six miles on blacktop, then go straight onto gravel when the blacktop takes a sharp bend to the right. Gravel will turn into dirt, but the signs are clear through the forest until you come out into the open meadow and the homestead. Using GPS, put in the address: 13249 Hanka Rd., Baraga, Michigan 49908. It is open and staffed by volunteers from Memorial Day through Labor Day, Thursdays through Sundays from noon to 4. Please visit www.SuperiorTapestry.com/sites for more information.

Fig. 10-2: Hanka Homestead Grounds

All of the homestead can be seen in this shot beginning with Sauna on the left, then the milk house, root cellar, farm house and some of the barns as you move from left to right.

Chapter 11 – In Bishop Baraga's Footprints

Fig. 11-1: Statue of Bishop Baraga

The statue of Bishop Baraga looks out over Keweenaw Bay, a place the venerable bishop often visited.

In 1969, a group of residents, headed by then Baraga County Clerk and author, Bernard Lambert, decided to move forward with their idea of creating a religious and historical shrine to Bishop Fredric Baraga. Their actions led them to work with metal sculptor Jack Anderson (who worked throughout the Midwest on large memorial statues) to fashion a likeness of Fredric Baraga, missionary priest to the Ojibwa and first Bishop of the Marquette Diocese.

Inspired by Lambert's book, *Shepherd of the Wilderness*, Anderson designed a thirty-five-foot statue of Baraga holding a seven-foot cross in one hand and twenty-six-foot snowshoes in the other, standing on a stainless steel "cloud" supported by five laminated curving wooden beams on top of five-foot concrete tepees—the five wood beams representing Baraga's first five missions. As Jack Anderson went to work in a building now called "The 9th Street Sub Station" in nearby Lake Linden in 1970, some of the inspiration from reading about Baraga's life must have entered the statue he was creating, and Statue came to know about the man he represented.

Statue felt Baraga's closeness to God in prayer. "His man" was born on June 29, 1797, in Malavas, Slovenia, a town in the northwest part of what used to be Yugoslavia. He was ordained a priest on September 21, 1823, and for the rest of his life, he was, first and always, a priest. Statue also felt Baraga's times of discouragement and loneliness over the years, as well as his joy in bringing so many souls to God.

As the sculptor formed Baraga's head, Statue remembered his first few years of priesthood. Baraga became known for bringing God's love and peace to those who came to him for confession. It was during that time that Fr. Fredric Rese, vicar of the Diocese of Cincinnati, visited Europe to find priests willing to serve as missionaries in the northern Midwest. Statue heard Baraga answer that call, and he arrived in Cincinnati on October 18, 1830. He already spoke German, French and English, and now studied the language of the Native People he hoped to bring into the Christian fold. Along the Lake Michigan shore of Michigan's Upper Peninsula (including the St. Ignace and Mackinac area), this would have been the Ottawa and Huron people, although the Ottawa, Ojibwa and Huron were all part of a greater group called the *Anishnaabe*, "First People," so their languages and customs were similar. The Ottawa and Huron people lived mostly in the Lake Michigan and Lake Huron areas, while the Ojibwa lived in the Lake Superior region.

As the hand of the statue holding the cross became real, Statue recalled May of 1831, when Baraga traveled with Bishop Fenwick to Arbre Choche in northern Lower Michigan. There, Baraga served an Ojibwa group and continued his study of their language. Statue felt a keen sense of pride as the man he represented began to write prayer books in the Ojibwa, preserving their language in written form and providing traditional prayers of the Catholic Church in the native language of his flock. Statue realized that because of Baraga's efforts, many Native People learned to read for the first time, in addition to preserving their language and culture. The "government schools" for Native People only allowed instruction in English, but Baraga helped them learn English and still keep their native language. Statue was proud that his man bucked the politics of that time.

While Baraga tromped around the wilderness, Statue learned that the Catholic Church set up the Diocese of Detroit in March of 1833. Statue's man came under that area while continuing his missionary work. From Arbre Croche, Baraga and Statue with him in spirit, traveled to Beaver Island, off the shore of Lake Michigan, near Manistique in the Upper Peninsula, then to Grand River where many Ottawa wintered. There, he was attacked one night by a group of drunken Native People. It was the beginning of his realization that drunkenness among his flock would be a constant problem. The French-Canadian fur traders had done Native People no favor when they introduced liquor in trade for furs. By July of 1835, Statue had been with Baraga as he established a mission at La Pointe and Fond du Lac, near Duluth, and L'Anse on Lake Superior.

Statue's creator, Jack Anderson, had an easy drive between Lake Linden and L'Anse, but Statue's man had to travel by canoe in the summer and snowshoes in winter—many miles of difficult trudging with danger and hardship all along the way. Statue experienced Baraga's delight when he arrived at Fond du Lac to find Pierre Cotte, who had been working with the Native People for a while. He already had a copy of Baraga's first Ojibwa language book of prayers and hymns and had taught that group to sing and pray.

Statue was with Baraga in spirit when he would rise as early as 2:30 or 3:00 a.m. to meditate and pray. His first concern was always for the Ojibwa he shepherded, to the point that he bought the land where several of his missions sat and then made a gift of it back to the Ojibwa. In the L'Anse area, they later formed the Keweenaw Bay Indian Community (KBIC), which is still there today. This allowed Baraga's flock to remain on their land when other clans were forced off theirs. It was in L'Anse that Statue heard that he acquired the name "The Snowshoe Priest."

These winter treks were not only long, but dangerous, since there were rarely any places to stop and take shelter for the night. Statue

felt the cold and hunger along with Baraga as he prepared places to
camp in the forest, often with only a few balsam boughs for shelter
from wind and snow. Statue remembered two remarkable, possibly
miraculous, journeys during those early years.

In 1846, while Fr. Baraga was on Madeline Island, part of the
Apostle Islands near Bayfield, Wisconsin, he received a message that
the Ojibwa at Grand Portage, Minnesota, were in great need of his
help during an epidemic. By land, the voyage would have been 200
miles and about a month of travel, but it was only about forty miles
across Lake Superior—less than one day's paddling. He set out in an
eighteen-foot canoe with one paddler, Louis Goudin. A storm came
up while they were out on the lake. Waves rose and the wind ripped
at their clothes. Louis paddled and Baraga prayed. Their first sight of
land was formidable, with no apparent place to land. "We will be
saved," Baraga reassured Louis. "Go straight on." Soon, they
spotted a calm river entering the lake and were able to land safely.
Baraga placed a cross there and prayed his thanks to God, calling the
place Cross River, which is near Schroeder, Minnesota. Many felt
that journey was a miracle.

Another time, Baraga needed to travel from La Pointe to
Ontonagon during spring break up. His companions and he set off
across the ice. Statue heard the fear spoken by those with Baraga
when a southeast wind came up, pushing the large ice flow they
walked on farther and farther from land. Again, Baraga assured
those with him, "We will be safe." He walked across the ice floe,
singing songs of faith. The wind shifted and pushed the ice gently to
shore. When all were safely on land, only a little way from their
destination, Baraga said, "See, we have traveled a great distance and
have worked very little."

It wasn't until 1852 that Fr. Baraga began to keep a diary. That
was when he first heard he would be named bishop of another new
diocese, because Michigan was growing in population. More
churches and priests would be needed to serve them. Statue surged
with both pride and humility when, on July 29, 1853, Rome
formally approved the establishment of the "Apostolic Vicariate of
Upper Michigan" and Baraga was appointed bishop. It was a huge
area, including all of Michigan's Upper Peninsula, northern
Wisconsin all the way to Duluth, Minnesota, but still including the
northern half of Michigan's Lower Peninsula, and parts of Canada

across the St. Mary's River at Sault Ste. Marie (Later, the areas in Wisconsin and Minnesota became part of other dioceses. The Upper Peninsula of Michigan would become the Diocese of Marquette).

Statue felt Baraga's conflicting emotions as he left his widely scattered flocks in the hands of a few other missionary priests to travel to Cincinnati and then Europe. He was now fifty-six years old and had been tramping around the wilderness for twenty years. Through Baraga, Statue felt how it was to sleep in a "real" bed and eat plenty of good food for a change. As part of that trip, he spent a good deal of time with the Society for the Propagation of the Faith, the Ludwig Mission Society in Munich, Germany and several other well-established groups to ask them for the money needed to continue his work. Very little cash money was available in his huge diocese. Almost a year passed before he returned.

Statue felt his spiritual weight increase with the Baraga's many new responsibilities. As a priest, he had many jobs: preaching, teaching, baptizing, marrying, tending the sick, burying the dead, hearing confessions, conducting services. Added to this, he now needed to govern the Catholic Church in that huge area. He performed confirmations, prepared men for the priesthood and ordained them. He also planned the building of new churches and saw that the plans were carried out, opened schools and tried to find capable teachers, keeping track of the whole flock and all those who strove to help him. And good help was not easy to find.

Michigan's Upper Peninsula now had immigrants of many nations, because thousands of people came to work in the iron, copper and timber industries. Baraga spoke multiple languages and often preached sermons in three languages on the same day; not many priests spoke all (or even two) of the languages needed. Some began eagerly, but then grew discouraged under the great challenges and asked to leave. Just as alcohol abuse was a problem with the Ojibwa, it also became a problem with some of the priests. Bishop Baraga had to reprimand, and sometimes dismiss, more than one priest for drunkenness. If he had previously traveled a lot around his huge area, now it was even more necessary—though there were larger, more comfortable ships now, at least from late May until November. Statue noted how often Baraga wrote in his diary about catching this or that steamship, or waiting for one to come so he could get to the next area he needed to visit. There were some days

Statue felt Baraga's longing to be a "simple missionary" again. There were also times when, even though a bishop, he took on the role of simple missionary priest because there was no one else there.

Statue couldn't help but smile as one man stated, "Bishop Baraga is made of iron. Nothing holds him back and he lives in places where an Indian would die of starvation." Statue saw the word "misère" written in his diary often, but "Thanks be to God," was penned an equal number of times. Statue felt that strong faith in every part of Baraga's being.

Some days, Statue would be "up" as Baraga received a large gift of money from European churches, or a small gift from one of his flock (such as a new pair of moccasins). Then, he would be "down" as he saw how poor some people were, coming to beg for a little food. He praised God each time he finished correcting the pages of another Ojibwa prayer book, but didn't like having to go to Detroit or Cincinnati, away from his people, to have these books printed.

Ups and downs came with the changes of weather, especially in late fall through the end of May. Sometimes, the boats did not come, or a bay or harbor became blocked with ice floes, keeping Baraga in a place when he needed to move on, or out of some place he needed to get to. It was necessary for him to visit some missions in the winter, because in summer, the people who lived there would be away fishing. An unexpected thaw might make these trips even more dangerous as rivers he expected to cross while they were frozen over suddenly were open and running. "Wood hauling day" was a constant theme in the winter. Year in, year out, "Misère," "Thanks be to God," back and forth, back and forth, and along with that, the rhythm of the church year: Lent, Easter, Pentecost, Holy Days, Christmas. Every year on July 4, the entry: "A day of sinning," because people mostly drank and danced on Independence Day.

Statue knew that even though travel became easier with steamships, it was still dangerous. Many a ship went down in Lake Superior with all those aboard. Statue noticed that Baraga struggled more with age, became tired, had trouble with his hearing off and on and spent days ill in bed. In 1861, he had to prepare and leave on a trip from Sault Ste. Marie to Cincinnati right after Easter, March 31, in order to arrive by late April. There were no boats coming to Sault Ste. Marie that early, so he went on foot for two and a half days to Mackinac. His snowshoes caused him pain, because the strings in the snowshoes had frozen hard to his moccasins. Statue could feel those terrible sores and the extra effort of struggling through deep snow without the snowshoes. The ice was still on Lake Huron when he arrived, so he and a companion rode on horseback five miles across the ice to the Lower Peninsula. Statue let out a long-held breath when Baraga and his companion arrived at the other shore safely and then cried with his man when he heard that his companion's horse fell through a crack in the ice upon his return.

From there, he marched many miles over rough roads through the wilderness, hoping to find a boat at Alpena; however, there was no boat yet. While he waited, Statue witnessed Baraga helping the people there with the planning of their new church building and conducting services. Several days went by, waiting, waiting. Statue knew Baraga's boredom, because he was a man of action, not one to sit around idle. Finally, on April 19, he boarded a fishing boat that would take him to Saginaw. They sailed perhaps thirty-eight miles to Harrisville and then went ashore for the night. The next morning, the wind was contrary—more waiting. On April 20, the other passengers decided to walk eighteen miles to the Sable River, but Statue knew Baraga could not walk even one mile now, so he remained in Harrisville. Finally, on April 22, the steam ship *City of Cleveland* arrived and Baraga took it to Detroit.

He arrived at the Cincinnati Council on time and was asked to preach at the cathedral there during the council. When the council ended on May 4 of that year, he returned to his many flocks. Each time he visited his original missions, now in the capable hands of other priests, Statue felt Baraga's nostalgia for his first years in the area. On and off deafness continued to plague him. In his diary, Baraga admitted that age was catching up with him, sometimes leaving him short of breath on walking journeys.

Statue remembered December 31, 1861, when Baraga wrote, "Very mild weather, no ice on the river (thirty-one years in America)." And in February 1862, he admitted in a letter, "I had scarcely gone a mile when I felt such heaviness and pressure in the chest that I thought I would have to fall. I recommended myself to God and walked on." In June of that year, Statue rejoiced while working with the Native People on Goulais Bay on the Canadian shore at Sault Ste. Marie as they labored "industriously" to build a wooden church for their community. Statue marveled that Baraga had been able to get hold of all the lumber and shingles needed and had personally seen to their delivery. He rejoiced even more in August when Baraga received $437.50 from the Leopoldine Society: "Thanks be to God a thousand times!" Sadness came in September that year when the seminary, in Milwaukee, Wisconsin, had to disband because adult, unmarried men were forced to go and fight during the Civil War.

In May of 1866, Statue welcomed Baraga's move from Sault Ste. Marie to Marquette, which was more central, for the seat of the diocese. Statue and Baraga suffered a terrible fall in October that year while in Cincinnati for the Second Provincial Council of Baltimore; however, he insisted on returning to Marquette, where he died January 19, 1868.

Statue was there in spirit when Father Jacker, one of the first priests to join Baraga in the north country, said in his public eulogy, "Thus ended a man whose purity of soul, whose mortified life and burning zeal, joined to uncommon talents and acquirements, faithfully and successfully employed in the service of God, and the most abandoned of his creatures; a man whose extraordinary achievements as a pioneer in Christianity will not allow his memory to pass away, as long as souls capable of appreciating so much virtue and excellency will live in this upper country, which has been the principle field of his labors and where his body now rests to await the summons for resurrection." (Biographical Introduction to *The Diary of Bishop Fredric Baraga*, pg. 28)

Statue was erected on land donated by the Patrick Ellico family. The Yalmer Mattila Contracting Company of Houghton worked on the base, and the copper made into brass in Statue came from the White Pine Mine, not far away. It was also donated. The Upper Peninsula Power Company gave free technical assistance. Evergreen Nurseries of Allegan, MI, donated landscaping. Statue looks year-round over the vistas of Keweenaw Bay, much in the way the man he represents did.

Since Then: Due to the ongoing work and prayers of many people, the Vatican declared Baraga a "Servant of God" in 1972—the first step of a long road to sainthood. In 2012, Pope Benedict XVI deemed him "Venerable"—the second step. Step three is one verified miracle, with the declaration of "Blessed," and a second verified miracle will bring "formal" sainthood.

Baraga's life brings to mind the words of a lesser-known Christmas carol, "Good King Wenceslas." Words for the carol were first composed in 1853 by John Mason Neale. The carol was composed for "Boxing Day," which is celebrated on December 26, the Feast of St. Stephen, as a day when people "box up" things they no longer need to be given to the poor.

> Good King Wenceslas looked out on the Feast of Stephen,
> Where the snow lay round about deep and crisp and even.
> Brightly shown the moon that night, though the frost was cruel,
> When a poor man came in sight gathering winter fuel.
>
> "Hither, page, and stand by me, if thou know'st it telling,
> Yonder peasant who is he, where and what his dwelling?"
> "Sire, he lives a good league hence, underneath the mountain,
> Right against the forest fence, by St. Agnes' Fountain."
>
> "Bring me flesh and bring me wine, bring me pine logs hither.
> Thou and I shall see him dine when we bare them thither."
> Paige and monarch forth they went, forth they went together,
> Thro' the rude wind's wild lament and the bitter weather.
>
> "Sire, the night is darker now, and the wind blows stronger.
> Fails my heart I know not how, I can go no longer."
> "Mark my footsteps, my good page, trod thou in them boldly.
> Thou shalt find the winter's rage freeze thy blood less coldly."
>
> In his master's steps he trod, where the snow lay dinted.
> Heat was in the very sod where the saint had printed.
> Therefore, Christian men, be sure wealth or rank possessing,
> Ye who will now bless the poor, shall yourselves find blessing.

Visitors may walk around the grounds of the shrine and see Statue at any time, but the gift shop is only open Thursday through Monday from 11 a.m. to 5 p.m. The shrine is located at: 17570 US 41, L'Anse, Michigan, 49946. Phone: 906-524-7021. Please visit www.SuperiorTapestry.com/sites for more info.

Chapter 12 – Chip of the Pines Casino

Fig. 12-1: a $1.00 casino chip from The Pines

Chip doesn't look like much, but he has a remarkable story to tell.

These days, Chip of the Pines Casino sits in a glass case with other memorabilia nearby. He's not that old, compared to other artifacts in the Baraga County Historical Museum, but he, and what he represents, played an important role in the ongoing struggle for Native People's rights and in the modern economic history of Baraga. He counts himself lucky to have survived, since all the others like him had to be destroyed due to important decisions in various courts, the most noteworthy being the United States Supreme Court. Chip is proud to be part of that legacy.

Chip is not worth any money now, but during the year and a half that people laid him on a blackjack table many times during the course of an evening, night and early morning at The Pines Casino, he was worth $1.00 in the game. He's rather handsome, he thinks, with his white painted identifying information on a black background. He was one of many such chips traded around, placed on the table and then scooped up by that round's winner. But the rest of them are gone now, leaving only Chip, a pamphlet or two and some volunteers to tell his story. Even the garage where Fred Dakota first set up his casino is gone, and the place where it once stood is now the Tribal Police Post.

A steady hand painted Chip's inscription onto the plain clay surface. That day, $1.00 was painted on his face, but other days, he might have had $5.00 or something higher, in the same place. The Pines Casino ran on a very limited budget. The walls told Chip that in the beginning, Fred Dakota and his wife had used poker chips bought in any store, and that sometimes, they checked as people entered to be sure they weren't sneaking in "outside" chips.

Chip's first night he heard, "All chips must be cashed in before you leave. They will be worthless tomorrow..." Every night, the same warning. After the 2 a.m. closing, Fred paid out to all patrons, handed some money to a couple of family members for dealing at the other tables and what was left over was his profit for that day. Fred's wife was the main bartender. Chip sensed that this was not the way other casinos operated, and he was curious about that.

By listening carefully every evening as the casino prepared to open, and again after it closed, Chip learned the answers to most of his questions. Fred had been born in 1937 to his barely sixteen-year-old mother, who left him in his grandmother's care for the first five years of his life. Then, his grandmother died of Tuberculosis and Fred was taken to the Catholic orphanage at Assinins. The nuns were kind, but his Catholic education included only English and nothing of his Ojibwa culture. His father, whom he had never known before, came to visit him a couple of times but left him at the orphanage. In 1949, his mother showed up with a stepfather, who often reminded Fred what they had to pay to get him out of the orphanage. Certainly, it was a less than idyllic childhood. Upon reaching adulthood, he worked here, there and the other place, ending up in Sault Ste. Marie.

Another evening, Chip heard that in 1955, Fred decided to join the Army, but ended up in the Marines because the Army recruiter was not around the day he showed up. Marine life was tough, but that was nothing new. He married his first wife in 1959, and, after a bit of bouncing from place to place, he got a job doing high iron work on buildings in Chicago. Ironically, he also spent some time working in a bow and arrow factory. At that time, Indians were paid less than other workers, and Fred related how often he heard others say, "We got an Indian working here," and not in a nice way. Fred ended up back in Baraga, where he worked nine years for Pettibone, a heavy equipment company, and became involved in the local tribal council. Then, he spent time on the Michigan Intertribal Council. This was unpaid, of course, and the bosses at Pettibone were not thrilled when Fred was frequently called to the phone during the day on tribal business, even though Fred told them repeatedly to call his home in the evening. Finally, he was able to earn around $6.00 per hour as the Tribe Chairman. By this time with his second wife, Fred had several new little Dakota mouths to feed.

Chip went from the "betting box" in front of a player to the dealer when the player went bust on a hand. He watched as the next player got a blackjack and he slid from the dealer to the winning player. Another round began and Chip and a few others sat in the betting box in front of the previous hand's winner. The Pines Casino had grown a little, now having more than one table. Chip caught a glimpse of drinks being loaded onto a tray and brought to his table. "His" player had a low card facing up, and, like everyone else, Chip did not know what the down-facing card was. His player tapped the table, once, twice, and then the player yelled an obscenity when the next card put him over "21." Chip and the rest of the man's bet went back to the dealer, who won the entire round. It was pretty much the same every night, to the point where Chip sometimes napped out of boredom until, after closing, he might hear more about Fred.

When people weren't talking, one wall sometimes filled in bits of information. In the early months of The Pines Casino, Fred readily admitted that he made mistakes but emphasized that he learned from those mistakes. After all, he'd only had a "formal" education through grade eight. One night, Chip heard Fred and his wife laugh at how the whole business got started. At some point (a year was not mentioned), the Baraga area Ojibwa tribe had gotten a grant from the Catholic Church's Campaign for Human Development. They used the money to hire a lawyer who helped them establish the tribe's right to enforce its own laws on reservation land. Fred began to attend more workshops on this and also pushed for the reservation to have its own police force. Somewhere in the mid-1970s, the Keweenaw Bay Indian Community became the first Ojibwa group in the state to accomplish this. KBIC then helped other tribes gain the same right, although because of prejudice, many people believed that Native People "couldn't do it." After eight years of legal work, another court decision was declared, the Jondreau Decision, which guaranteed hunting and fishing rights on reservation land. Through all that time, Fred was still working at Pettibone. Cliff often heard Fred tell others, "People in the United States don't want to face the truth of our own history."

Cliff heard about tough times on the reservation at Baraga. Grants only went so far and then ended. The tribal construction company could not manage to make a profit. Then Fred heard about how Native People in other states were earning money with "Big Bucks Bingo." He proposed to the tribal council that they change reservation law to allow for this type of game. Helene Welsch, a sharp, elderly lady on the council, suggested that they go farther and include casino gambling in their reservation code. Cliff heard Fred chuckle recalling that, back then, the Bureau of Indian Affairs had a habit of not taking any action on things for months at a time, and if they "did nothing," then in fourteen days, a proposal sent to them by an individual tribe automatically became law!

Chip wanted to cheer, but of course, no one would have heard him, except maybe the wall.

KBIC made enough with Big Bucks Bingo to pay off its debts, and Fred continued to be voted head of the council. But, by this time, Pettibone had left Fred behind. Unemployment compensation wasn't nearly enough to feed five children. Fred's brother-in-law had a two-car garage on tribal land and was willing to let Fred use it. Fred applied to the council for a casino license. The council laughed at Fred's idea of his own casino, but they gave him the license. Chip could see it displayed on the garage wall and beamed with pride. The only banker who would give Fred a loan to get started was a friend, who granted a $10,000 personal loan.

The loan was used to remodel the garage—a bar on one side, one table (with "the green" purchased from Las Vegas), several decks of cards, the first unofficial chips, beer and so on. Fred and his wife put flyers on cars in the grocery store parking lot and on community bulletin boards, advertising the opening of The Pines Casino, New Year's Eve, 1983.

"Boy, that was scary," Chip heard Fred say one night as they counted the money. They had worried that the FBI, the Michigan state police or Baraga county sheriff might show up to challenge them before they could even get started. But the first night was very successful, and, in a few months, Fred had paid off the personal loan.

Soon, Chip watched as Fred added more tables to the garage. Each night, the garage filled quickly with people wanting to play for a dollar or two a hand. By closing time, the room had a haze of smoke, and beer spilled on the floor stuck to the bottoms of shoes and boots, then got tracked out the door—a mess to mop up. The Pines needed more room to expand.

Fred, laughing as he came in one evening to get ready to open, told the others that now that The Pines Casino was making regular deposits, the bank was anxious to loan the casino more money. He only wanted $60,000? Couldn't he use $100,000?

All the talk was cheerful as a new, larger building went up on nearby Ojibwa land. Chip, the other chips, all the equipment and the casino license shared the excitement as they were packed up and moved to the new building with new tables for other casino card games, slot machines and other trappings of a "real" casino. The new, improved Pines Casino opened July 4, 1984. All was going well until the council declared that the casino license given to Fred for the garage location would **not** transfer to the new building and reported Fred to the United States Attorney General's office. Chip wondered if the Tribal Council might have been just a bit jealous of Fred's success.

Chip listened to all the discussions as Fred fought for the right to stay open. His attorney, Hunter Watson of Calumet, faced off with the tribe's attorney, a man named Garfield. Both parties agreed that they did not want to have to go to a jury trial, so they reached a compromise. Since Michigan law already allowed non-profits to have casino gambling three days per year, and other tribes already had gambling (Fred Dakota was not the first), he should be able to continue. And so, The Pines continued in operation.

Chip felt their pain as Fred explained a new problem to his wife and employees. According to the final court decision, other tribal casinos were non-profit, and since Fred Dakota was in business to make a profit, his personal operation would have to shut down! "This little Indian got his butt kicked.... The whole system is corrupt, crazy... Somebody's got to break the ice, and it takes a lot of guts.... If you believe in sovereignty, you exercise sovereignty (Jan. 30, 2012, "Interview with Fred Dakota," with Russell M. Magnaghi, p. 40)."

On the last night before The Pines Casino closed for good, Chip ended up in the hands of a man from "Downstate," the Upper Michigan term for the Lower Peninsula, or all areas "below" the Big Mac Bridge. This man had stopped in on his way to Houghton to play a few hands of blackjack. All chips were to be collected and destroyed after that last day. The man, when down to his last chip, decided it might make a nice souvenir and slipped Chip into his pocket. He often showed Chip to friends and family, but Chip spent most of his time in a drawer those years. He knew nothing of what happened at the casino after that until, on another trip to the Upper Peninsula, that same man walked into the Baraga County Historical Museum and handed Chip to them.

Afterword: What Chip Did Not Know

The increase in the number of Native American operated casinos boiled down to three factors (History of Gaming in Baraga County, PDF):

1. The 1976 United States Supreme Court decision in Bryan vs. Itasca Co., which stated that tribes had the right to rule their own civic affairs.

2. The Indian Reservation Act of 1976, which encouraged tribes to pursue economic development.

3. The fact that during the 1970s, more states began to legalize gambling permits for bingo and non-profit "casino nights" for fundraising purposes.

KBIC took over operation of the casino as a nonprofit to remain legal under Michigan law. Many people were concerned about the vices that casino gambling might bring to a community. However, in Baraga County, 2% of the casino's annual profit goes to local government, schools, fire departments, law enforcement and local non-profits. Their profits have also made it possible to begin other tribally-owned businesses, such as a gas station, hardware and lumber stores, marina, campground and a solid waste transfer station. The tribe has the largest payroll in Baraga County, employing over 500 people. Baraga County has seen other benefits, such as funding for water systems and housing, lower unemployment, social service funding, less reliance on federal funds and grants and pride in their heritage and culture.

The importance of The Pines Casino and its closure is not in its being "first" but in its influence on other court cases and the fact that the Keweenaw Bay Indian Community is the largest and oldest reservation in Michigan. It may never have happened if Fred Dakota hadn't had the courage to take the first step.

You can visit Chip at the Baraga County Historical Museum, 803 US 41 S. Baraga, Michigan, 49908. The museum is normally open Thursdays and Fridays, 11 a.m. to 3 p.m., from June 6 through Aug. 30. You can visit in the off-season by making an appointment, contact then via email: baragacountyhistory@gmail.com. This is an all-volunteer organization, so be patient when awaiting a reply. Visit www.SuperiorTapestry.com/sites for more info.

Fig. 12-2: Baraga County Historical Museum on a summer day (2020)

Chapter 13 – Tools of the Home Speak

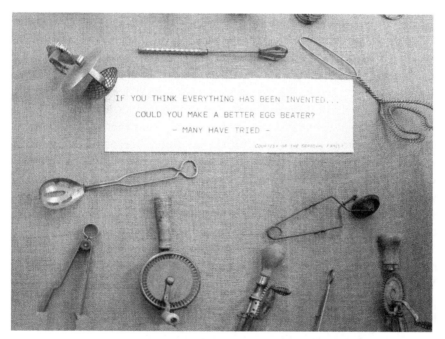

Fig. 13-1: Copper Range Historical Museum Objects

Here are some of the objects in the Copper Range Museum that became characters in this chapter.

On the main street in the town of South Range, Michigan, stands a red brick building filled with objects from everyday life during the Copper Boom days of the early 20th century. It was the most modern building in town when it was first built to house the South Range Bank. Now, every nook, cranny, space (under and on counters) and wall space is filled with what it was like "back in the day." There are wash tubs, ice picks, darning eggs, dishes, kitchen gadgets, things made from other things in "Early Copper Country Recycling," a room set up as a general store, a rag-rug loom, manikins dressed in period clothing and a thousand other things, each with its own story. If you close your eyes for a moment and open your imagination, you can hear them speak.

One wall display shows every kind of eggbeater you could think of, and more. Of course, some are fancier than others, looking down—literally—on those "at the bottom," and, like women of every age since women began talking to each other, they gossip. So do the male-oriented objects.

"Oh, I can tell you, I've whipped up a million meringue pies in my life," said one of the upper-class beaters. "My mistress was known for the very best tea parties in town! Every week, the finest ladies came dressed in their *best* and sat in our parlor sipping tea and eating my lovely pies from the *best* china money could buy."

"Yes, I'm sure, but did the mistress whip that meringue? Or was it really a servant girl from a home like mine?" retorted the slotted spoon who also had beaten a good many eggs. "I believe my owner was the young woman who held you in her hands and worked for your mistress. I can tell you how good she was because her hand was strong enough, and she had enough energy to beat up an angel food cake with me! You know that takes a **lot** of whipping."

"Would you two stop trying to one-up each other? All of us beat a lot of eggs, omelets, cakes, lemon custards and everything else. Women rich and poor used us. Now we're all here trying to help people, over a hundred years later, understand what kitchens were like before electricity changed everything. None of us is better than the other," stated yet another of the eggbeaters.

Several objects around them nodded their agreement, including a nearby Victrola wind-up record player, whose job had been to provide music in a home. The two haughty eggbeaters glared at each other and lapsed into silence.

"May I entertain you all this evening?" asked a polite fishing bobber at the other end of the wall.

"Yes, please do," said several objects at once.

"The man who made me was very poor—as you see, I'm simply a cork from an old bottle with a twig stuck through me. Even though I'm here with these Great Depression era things, I was made much earlier in the century. My man and maker attached his fishing line to me and caught a whole lot of fish that he brought home to his parents. As he grew up, he didn't want to take one of those dangerous underground jobs pushing tramcars in the copper mines, so he worked at every job he could find for a day, a week – whatever—and he never gave up. You see, he was very much in love with a particular young lady. Unfortunately, she was the daughter of the mine captain. They had met by chance at a church social. He talked about her endlessly, while I floated on the surface of the water with his hooked line beneath me. When a fish bit at his hook, it would pull me under, and he'd jerk the line to set the hook and catch a fish. Anyway, every chance he got, he'd try to be where she would be. Smiles passed between them. Then, conversations—short ones— followed by friendship. She didn't seem to care who he was, because she could tell he was sincere. That mattered more to her than money.

"I bet her father didn't like that very much," said one of the skis made from barrel stays. "My owner was thrown off more than one porch over on what people called 'the right side of the tracks.'" The ski's mate explained that long, thin cross-country skis were one of the ways to get around in the woods during the winter. Faster than snowshoes, they slid along the top of the snow. Those who lived far from town found they also came in handy to check trap lines or snares meant to catch small game for the stew pot—quite a difference from today's use of skis for winter recreation.

"No, he didn't," Cork Bobber continued. "But by this time, the two had grown so much in their friendship (which had actually turned into love) that they began to sneak out to meet each other. She'd excuse herself to the outhouse during the pastor's Sunday sermon, and he'd do the same. They knew that would get them at least fifteen minutes. Then, she'd go out to do a bit of shopping and 'run into' him on the way...love always finds a way."

"Did her father catch them?" the haughty eggbeater asked, now quite interested in the tale. "Once my master caught his daughter with some low-life scum...oh, excuse me, some less fortunate young man, and he locked her in a room in the attic for a month!"

"No, actually, he never did catch them, until after it was too late. You see, these two young people thought up a most careful plan. She saved all the change from the shopping trips her mother sent her on, and he saved every extra dime he earned, finally getting a steady job with a logging company. They planned for months and months. His job did take him away from town for several months in the winter, but they managed to write and pass letters to each other through a mutual friend. I wasn't around to see when he eloped with her (he did not have me in his back pocket that night), but after two days, while I waited in the log cabin he built in the woods near where he worked, he carried his bride over the cabin's threshold."

From across the room, the usually quiet Stereoscope spoke up. "I can tell you what happened that night," she said. Because Stereoscope had never spoken up before, she ended up introducing herself and what she was before all the objects heard the rest of the story. She was a device into which one put a cardboard "slide" with two copies of a photograph on it. When one looked into the device (somewhat like looking into binoculars), the effect was that the two photos blended into one, but with depth in the image. When you look at a photograph, you see something flat, but when looking through the device, people felt as though they were looking at the real object or place. Stereoscope also explained that she was often used as evening entertainment for a group. The host, or hostess, would describe a picture and then pass Stereoscope around for everyone to look at one photograph after another while discussing the scenes. A whole box of photos sat beside her for museum visitors to try her out.

"Anyway," Stereoscope went on, "I sat on a table by a window at the back of the house. My young mistress' bedroom was right above. One night, a young man arrived with a ladder—right outside the window in front of me. I heard the softest thump ever as the young man propped the ladder against the wall of the house. This was followed by whispers as he climbed up. Down came one, and then another, traveling case, followed by my young lady. A noise from another upstairs bedroom made them freeze on the spot—holding their breath lest they be discovered. When it was quiet again, she finished climbing down the ladder and into his waiting arms. Oh, what a long kiss they shared!"

"A long kiss? Oh, my!" declared one of the darning eggs. The Old Darning Egg echoed this with "tsk-tsk" noises.

Every object in the place knew that a "proper" man or woman did not kiss in public—at all! More often than not, that kiss at the church alter after the preacher said, "You may now kiss your bride," was a couple's first kiss. Anything else was the subject of gossip and considered a sinful scandal.

Stereoscope continued, "Well, they were in love, and their elopement would be a scandal anyway, so why not kiss? I heard him whisper that he had a horse and cart waiting and they would go straight away to the Houghton County Courthouse. It would be a fairly long ride, and they'd still have to wait for the courthouse to open in the morning so the local judge could marry them. Then, they would ride many more miles, arriving by nightfall, at the home he'd built for her."

"I bet all hell broke loose when her father found her gone the next morning," said Darning Egg.

"Absolutely! Oh, the shouting that morning," Stereoscope said. "The master left straight away, riding his fastest horse, but when he returned that afternoon, his head hung. He told his wife that he asked the sheriff to go find them, but was told they'd already seen the judge, and he didn't know where they'd gone. That sheriff had the nerve to smile at me about it! You know who won't get **my** vote next fall! And if she ever comes back here, you're not to give her anything! 'She's no longer my daughter!' my master yelled, shaking his finger at his wife."

"How did it turn out for the two of them?" Darning Egg asked.

"Very well," Bobber said. "Of course, at first, they didn't have much, but he taught her to fish, and she used me often to catch their dinner while he worked in the woods. By the following summer they had a beautiful baby boy. He worked hard and got a better job back in town, then bought a business and ended up quite well off. They'd come out to that log cabin with children (then grandchildren) during the summer and fish, using better bobbers than I was, but that was okay. I remained on the fireplace mantle many years in a place of honor. They often talked about how they reconciled with her father on their fifth wedding anniversary—after all, the young man had proven himself to be a good husband in every way."

Nods and sighs from many of the museum's collections ended that night's entertainment.

The following evening, Darning Egg, and her various sized sisters and cousins, explained her role in the lives of the people. "Well, you see, in our day, people didn't throw a thing away when it wore out, especially socks. When a thin spot appeared, usually in the heel or toe of a sock, the rest of the sock was still in very good condition. A woman would put my curved edge into the place on the sock that needed mending. She usually did this in the evening while listening to other members of the family talk about their day, or what they heard from the neighbors, or what was going on around town, or around the country. I would take the place of a person's toe or heel so the sock retained its proper shape. Women always had quite a collection of colors and thicknesses of darning yarns and threads, some wool and some cotton, so they could match the new thread to the color and thickness of the old as closely as possible. They would start a new line of thread far enough from the worn spot that they could anchor it in an area that was not worn. Lines of thread would go side-to-side of the hole, and then they would weave threads in the other direction over and under, over and under, until the hole was filled with this makeshift, newly-woven fabric. Sometimes, I filled the heel of a sock that had already been darned once or twice before. People who don't have much money make things last as long as possible."

"It wasn't exactly an exciting job, but very necessary," added a tiny Darning Egg. "I was used in smaller socks, usually a child's. The man of my house worked in one of the copper mines. Boots could chafe a foot and form blisters if a sock was worn, so it was very important for socks to be thick and smooth. Sometimes, we did hear interesting news. Often, the man of the house would read the newspaper while his wife mended—both of them by the light of kerosene lamps if the sun had already gone down. I was in a poorer household, so sometimes the newspaper was already a week old—one neighbor having passed it on to the next."

"What was your favorite type of news to hear?" asked Ice Pick.

"I never cared much for politics or events across the ocean I knew nothing about. The type of news that I liked most was what excited the children, and it came each summer when the circus would roll into town in its very own train. Those children would jump and dance, crying, 'Please, please, may we go to the circus this year?' Oh, how they wanted to see the trained elephants and watch the ladies on the flying trapeze in person—not just on the posters they saw in every store window between the school and home. The circus was the high point of the summer—even more than the 4th of July. Of course, their father would object at first, saying it would be too much money, but the children would beg and beg, offering to do extra chores. That particular year, they even went out on the streets, asking neighbors if they could do something to earn a few pennies or a nickel to help with the ticket price. And, of course, the day before the final performance, their father would manage to find enough extra money to take the entire family. Then, the jumping and laughing would begin and last long after they had come home sticky from eating candied apples, even long after the circus had left town. There is such joy in the laughter of children."

Ice Pick and Ice Shaver agreed that they liked summer best, too, since that was when they were most used. Every week, the ice man came around with his wagon to put a new block of ice in the ice box, which helped keep food from spoiling. Sometimes, on a hot afternoon, the lady of the house would hit the main block with Ice Pick to break off a chunk. Then, Shaver would go to work, shredding the chunk into a sort of rough snow, which would be put in a cup. The mother of the house would pour a bit of maple syrup over it for an icy cold treat for the children. The whole museum smiled that evening as they went to sleep.

There are hundreds of stories such as these to be heard in the Copper Range Museum. Imagine as many as you can as you look around. If you're unsure of what you hear, simply ask that day's volunteer, who will probably be able to answer your questions or fill in the details. Come by and visit.

Copper Range Historical Museum, 44 Trimountain Ave., P.O. Box 148, South Range, Michigan, 49963, ph. 906-482-6125

Open June through September each year, Tuesdays through Fridays, noon to 3 p.m. Hours may vary since all personnel are volunteers. Please visit www.SuperiorTapestry.com/sites for more info.

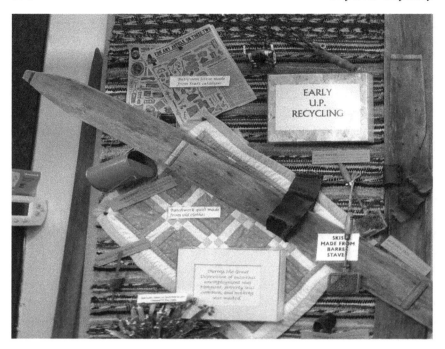

Fig. 13-2: More Objects from the museum

Fig. 13-2: Copper Range Historical Museum (2020)

Chapter 14 – The Quincy Mine Man Car

Fig. 14-1: The Man Car today

Empty for many years, Man Car greets visitors, who come to learn the area's history of the old mine.

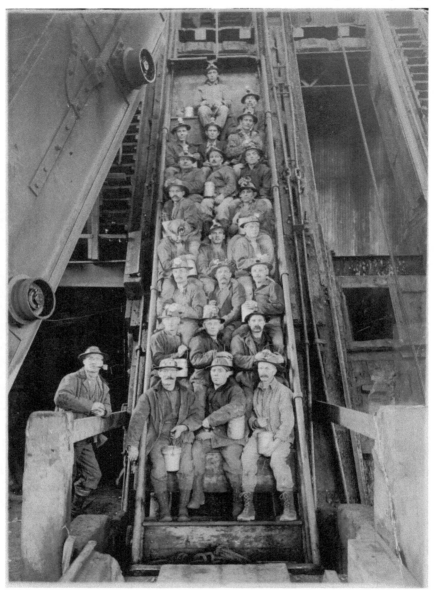

Fig. 14-2: The Man Car, filled with men going down for their shift

Photo courtesy of Michigan Technological University Archives and Copper Country Historical Collections, Nara Collection.

The day Man Car was installed in Quincy Mine in 1892, he knew he had one of the most important jobs to do in the entire operation. There were skip cars at the mine whose job was to bring copper ore up the mine shaft. Man Car was new, sleek and very modern for his day—a long, narrow version of a skip car. He had ten bench seats. Carrying three men to a bench, Man Car could transport thirty men at a time down or up the shaft. Before he started work, people went up and down in a car with two "compartments," one on top of the other, each about the size of a six-ton skip car and only carrying twenty men.

His wheels rode on the same track as the skip cars down a 45° angle deep into the mine. He, the new man car, could go down and up in less time than the old as well. Men began to get in and sit on his benches. The commands came, "Hold still! Heads down! Arms to your side!" Once loaded, a man next to the shaft pulled a bell cord. This signaled the steam hoist operator in another building, quite a distance away, that he could begin the descent. Thump! Then the descent into the dark. Gaining speed now, wind whistling in the faces of the miners, grinding and shrieking sounds of the wheels on the track, the temperature increasing the lower Man Car went. Another thump at the bottom. Stopped.

Men beginning their shift got out and headed down tunnels lit only by the tiny lights from the "sunshine" lamps on the fronts of their helmets to guide them. It was 80° and humid at that depth—compared to the crisp fall day at the surface. Other men, having finished their shift, piled in for the ride up. The sound of the bell, THUMP, rising to the surface, unloading, loading... Then more down, more up, more down, more up, until all the men were where they were supposed to be. "A good first day," the shift boss said. "Record time. This new Man Car works good; another day with no incidents or injuries. This one ought to have an even better safety record than the old one." Man Car took a deep, satisfying breath.

The thick rope cable was unhooked from the top of Man Car. Workers shifted him to one side of the shaft, maneuvered the skip car into place, and reattached the cable. Down went the empty skip car, then up it came, loaded with copper ore, which was hauled all the way to the top of the shaft house to be dumped into a series of sorters—rock with no copper down one shoot, smaller pieces of rock into another to be crushed into sand, then transported in rail cars down from the top of the high ridge above the town of Hancock to the smelting facility on the shore of Portage Lake. Shouting, clunking and rumbling filled the rock house.

Man Car was in awe of everything he saw that day, for he understood little of it. None of the equipment around him had any time to talk, so the only way Man Car could learn about himself or his job was to listen to the men and the bosses throughout the day. He did notice that the skip car went up and down even faster than he did, moving at 1000 feet per minute. The bell signals were different, too, when the skip car was hauling ore up, then going back down, empty. At the end of the shift, the skip car came off the track and Man Car slid into place on the track. Men climbed in and his job began once again. A reminder from the shift boss, "No tools going down, nothing that might stick out or snag in the shaft. Arms at side, heads down. Let's make this a safe ride."

Over the first several weeks that Man Car was on the job, he saw that sometimes—usually in some emergency—one or more men took their chances riding up or down in the skip car, their faces ashen— from the riskier ride, or from whatever the emergency was. Man Car never knew. There was a day, however, that he heard the shift boss talk about some problems that could happen. The steam hoist operator, in the building many feet away, could not see problems with the skip car or Man Car. Those who could see possible problems could not control the movement up or down of either car. That was what made those bell signals so important. Because of the depth of the shaft, and the science of the way tons of rock had to be hoisted up a great distance, the steam hoist engine house had to be that far away.

What are those possible problems? Man Car wondered.

As if they could hear him, the shift boss and another man began to discuss this. A piece of rock might fall out of the skip car, or come loose from the sides of the shaft, or be accidentally knocked down the shaft when the tram cars full of ore from various stopes and levels arrived at the shaft to be dumped into the skip car. Quincy Mine had many levels, all connected by the shaft going up and down, stopping at one or another when needed. The stopes were the tunnels branching off from each level. The one-and-a-half-inch diameter rope pulling both Man Car and the skips up and down might break, sending ore or men crashing down to their deaths. Man

Car shuddered at the thought—crashing would end him, too. One hundred or more loads of ore a day; twenty six to thirty times up and down per day with Man Car. Bosses watched him constantly. He was relieved when he heard the bosses say that there were special safety catches along the shaft to help in emergency braking. More than once a week, bosses inspected the rope and applied special lubricants. Man Car learned they expected a rope to last about three years. He heard them say that halfway through that time, the rope would be turned end to end so it wore evenly.

Over the years, Man Car began to understand many types of emergencies. The bells would ring; a skip car went down empty as fast as possible and then rose slowly, bearing the crushed and broken body (or bodies) of some miner who was in the wrong place at the wrong time. Rock from the hanging wall (the ceiling of a tunnel) sometimes fell on men; blasting went wrong; equipment failed... Some of those broken bodies managed to survive, never to work again. Others were already dead when they came up or died later of their injuries. Man Car sometimes heard grumbling from the miners about safety issues, but they never spoke loud enough for the bosses to hear. As Man Car listened, he found that many languages were spoken by these men, so he had to listen carefully for a language he understood. Sometimes it was difficult to make out words spoken with different accents.

Once, he heard a man tell his eighteen-year-old son, "Don't complain if you want keep job. I know man complained. Got fired. His name go on 'black list.' Nobody else hire him." The young man nodded. Of course, the mining companies denied that there were such lists, but there it was—some men were fired and could not find other jobs.

New drills arrived in 1911, an improvement in the company's eyes. Although still very heavy, the one-man drill was lighter than the two-man drill and required only one worker to operate. In the eyes of the miners, it was dangerous, because that man was out of sight of other workers. If something happened, no one was nearby to help him. Plus, half of the drill operators lost their jobs. Grumbling increased among the men and it was no longer hushed in the presence of bosses.

All that discontent blew up one day in July 1913. The men went on strike, and suddenly everything at the mine went silent. Man Car could finally ask equipment around him if they knew what was going on. The walls of the shaft spoke up first.

"Way back in the mid-1860s, when this mine was new, men climbed up and down ladders to work the mines. It took a very long time at shift changes. Men coming up groaned about sore muscles and the long climb. In cold weather, the rungs of the ladder near the top would be icy. Even with gloves and heavy boots, it was difficult to grip the rungs. Many a man fell to his death. Then, Joseph Rawlings came to this area from Cornwall, England. He was very young, but a brilliant machinist, and explained how mines in Europe used what was called a 'man engine' to get workers down and up."

"Was a man engine like me?" Man Car asked.

"Not quite. It was more of a mechanical ladder. Men stood on a one-foot-square platform that moved up six to ten feet at a time. Then, they stepped on the one next to it and went up the next, and so on. Each man stepped in turn behind the other until they were up and out of the mine or down to work their shift. This saved the men's strength; men even worked to a much older age than before. But it was a slow process."

Shouting interrupted their conversation as angry striking workers blocked the doors, keeping out others who still wanted to work. Company men shouted back—something about having to keep the pumps working to stop ground water from flooding the tunnels. If that happened, nobody might ever be able to work again. The striking miners allowed the pumping. Not long after, the hum of water pumps could be heard, but it wasn't so loud that Man Car could not hear Shaft speak.

Man Car asked about the many languages he heard.

"Immigrants have been coming here for many, many years," Shaft said. "These men were desperate for any kind of work to feed their families. They came thousands of miles from Cornwall, England and Ireland first, then Germany, all the Scandinavian countries—especially Finland. Others came from Italy, Poland, Russia, Croatia and many other countries in Eastern Europe. That's why you hear so many different sounds in their talk. I can't begin to name them all. Even though their wages are low—some call them slave wages—these families are still better off than wherever they came from."

Man Car sat silent.

Shaft continued. "I remember the oldest days, before the railroads were built, when ships were the only way to get supplies in and copper out. Sometimes, winter storms would start early and the last of the supplies, including barrels of flour, dried beef and pork, smoked herring, tobacco, lard, dried apples, butter, sugar, tea and coffee would not arrive. There were a few winters people nearly starved. All that is better now. Even though a lot of food and goods are still shipped in, there are farms here to provide some food locally. And train engines have plows on the front in the winter to remove the snow."

"Company stores sell all these things to their workers, so mining companies end up making a profit that way, too, getting most of the money back that they paid out in wages. True, wages have gone up a little over the years, and there are other stores to compete with company stores, but that is another thing these men are angry about. They are always in debt to company stores and other merchants who will give them credit."

"I never realized how hard the men had it," Man Car remarked. "So, while they are 'free' to leave, they really aren't 'free.' No wonder they are so angry."

"This mine is one of the richest in the area. I hear them call me 'Old Reliable'," Shaft said. "But the deeper I go, the less copper there is in the ore. I've heard Quincy Mining Company is having a hard time competing with open pit copper mines out west."

Shaft was quiet for a few minutes and then added, "Oh, I forgot to say that by 1890, the Man Engines had gone about as deep as they could. That's where the idea for you was born."

The strike ground on through the rest of the summer of 1913, into the fall and through the winter. Mine operators never thought the workers could last that long, but they did. Rumors flowed freely, along with reports of violence, murder and beatings by company-hired deputies. Man Car and Shaft despaired when they heard of the deaths of seventy-four people in the Italian Hall in Calumet on Christmas Eve—most of them children. Shaft and Man Car never did hear all the details of that.

Finally, on Easter Sunday of 1914, the members of the union voted to go back to work. They were beaten, but not all was lost. The mining companies claimed the union and the strike had nothing to do with it, and that they were planning to increase wages and

lessen work hours, anyway. The men did "win" an eight-hour day, a
five-day week and an increase of fifty cents a day in pay. Man Car
was glad to have workers oil his and Skip Car's wheels, lubricate a
new rope cable and other start-up chores. He and Shaft were glad to
get back to work. They sensed this in the miners riding down the
shaft, too. They weren't happy, but they accepted what had to come.

Man Car sensed that even though the men still disliked the one-
man drill, they realized that it did mean producing more ore. A few
years later, during World War I, the men were more content when
they received another wage increase. At Christmas in 1919, Man Car
heard a lot of happy talk about the company gift to all the workers'
children: candy, gifts from Santa, ice cream and a Cornish choir
singing carols. But all of them—men, machines and shaft—sensed
deep down that the "golden age" of copper had ended. It was only a
matter of time until they would be silenced forever.

Man Car happily carried men up and down the shaft for a couple
more decades, but he could hear the mine bosses talking about the
high cost of getting copper out of the ground—the mine went down
over a mile now—and the drop in the price of copper. The end was
near. Man Car felt grateful for every day he worked.

Old Reliable ceased operations in September 1945. Man Car
stood silent, mourning his and everyone else's position. While
Quincy Mining Company continued to make a profit through
reworking of the stamp sands at Mason on Torch Lake—which
lasted until 1967—Man Car had nothing to do. He stared through
cracks in the rock house walls as most of the Quincy Mine buildings
on top of the ridge fell into ruin. Rust ate away at him.

However, the people of the area worked to save Man Car. People
from all over the world come to visit Quincy Mine, Man Car and the
huge Steam Hoist during the summer months. Man Car is proud that
the place is a cooperating site with the Keweenaw National
Historical Park. Come and visit him and see.

Man Car would like to leave you with the words of a poem first
published in the *Portage Lake Mining Gazette* on February 4, 1865.
He was told that the original poem, from the front page of that
paper, may be viewed on microfilm at Michigan Technological
University Archives and Copper Country Historical Collections.
Man Car says that even though the poem is before his time, and
about a man engine, he feels it speaks of him, too.

Song of the Man Engine

Ho, ho for my arms of wood and steel
That are always strong and never can feel
The weakness that creeps o'er the muscles of men
(Though they fashioned mine by some curious plan,)
As he trembling clings to the ladder's round
Two hundred fathoms underground!

Weary with toil for one third of the day
I hear their foot falls echoing this way;
Put on thy strength, oh arms of mine
Carry them where the sun doth shine
One by one they come without sound
From two hundred fathoms underground!

Hammers and drills they left behind,
Down in the caves their strength hath mined.
And quickly their fears all pass away
As swiftly they rise to the upper day—
Trusting the friend whose arms they've found
Two hundred fathoms underground!

Then Ho! Again for my arms of steel
And lo, for my rods and strong-toothed wheel
Ho! Ho! Oh man! For the man engine
I'll save your strength if you'll manage mine
And ne'er shall you reel on the ladder's round
Two hundred fathoms underground.

Visit the Quincy Mine Hoist and Man Car at: 49750 US41
North, Hancock, Michigan 49930 ph. 906-482-3101. For more info
please visit www.SuperiorTapestry.com/sites.

Chapter 15 – A Bridge Across

New Portage Lake bridge (lift type) built 1958 & 1959. Opened for
traffic December 20, 1959. Old Portage Lake bridge survey began
in 1896 by James P. Edward. Steel bridge ready for traffic early
spring of 1897. Wrecking of old bridge started Dec. 21, 1959.
Picture taken Dec, 9, 1959 by J. Harry Reeder. Looking south.

Fig. 15-1: New Bridge (right) and Old Bridge (left)

Caption: Bridge is seen here next to Old Bridge shortly before Old Bridge
was demolished and Bridge opened in 1959. Photo used courtesy of
Michigan Technological University Archives and Copper Country Historical
Collections.

Fig. 15-2: 1ˢᵗ Bridge Between Houghton and Hancock

The first bridge between the twin cities of Houghton and Hancock. The year the photo was taken is unknown, but it had to have been prior to 1897. Photo used courtesy of Michigan Technological University Archives and Copper Country Historical Collections, Nara Collection.

Bridge became conscious of his purpose as soon as the first sheet pilings were pounded into the bed of Portage Lake in 1957. He knew at once that he would become a bridge, a unique bridge. He also knew that he was not the first bridge to be built in this place, because he could see an older bridge near him, clogged with vehicle traffic.

When those first pilings reached the lake bottom, he learned from the mud that there had been an even earlier bridge across this narrow arm of Portage Lake between the twin towns of Houghton and Hancock. Portage Lake had long been a shortcut through the Keweenaw Peninsula. Native People had paddled through the marshes at each end and through Portage's various narrow arms and wide main portion for a long time before new people found the immense copper deposits along the spine of the peninsula.

Mud also said that as more people came to dig copper from the earth in the ridge above where Bridge would be, they dredged out those marshes to form channels for larger boats and ships to pass through what they named the Keweenaw Waterway. This sheltered passage off Lake Superior, running from the southeast at Jacobsville to the northwest at "the lily pond" not far from McLain St. Park, was often a safe harbor for all sizes of ships and boats during Lake Superior's mighty storms. During the course of a hundred plus years, the channels were dredged deeper and wider to accommodate larger ships. The land on the Hancock side of Portage Lake became a man-made island. People had to get back and forth from one side to the other.

By 1853, several ferry boats crossed back and forth carrying people, horses, carriages and goods. When the lake froze in winter, people simply walked or rode across the ice with horses and sleighs. This was barely a year after Ransom Sheldon built the first building on the Houghton side. Mud told Bridge how quickly the two towns had grown around the copper mines. Mud also said that the first wooden bridge was built by two brothers-in-law, James P. Edwards and George C. Sheldon, Ransom's son. They had received permission to put in a toll bridge. The tolls paid would pay for the cost of the bridge and later provide the builders with a profit. The center span of that swing bridge opened on huge hinges when a ship needed to pass. Giant wheels on circular tracks turned the hinges of the center span to open and close it. Traffic began to flow over it in 1876. The toll for that bridge was less than the ferries charged. Ferries soon went out of business.

Mud said, "Those ferry owners complained a lot about that."

"Will I be a toll bridge?" Bridge asked.

"I don't think so," Mud answered. "That metal swing bridge started out as a toll bridge, but then I heard that in 1895, its owners sold it to the county and there was never a toll after that."

Bridge looked thoughtfully at the old iron swing bridge. It had two lanes of traffic on its upper deck—one for each direction—and a railroad level underneath. The huge wheels used to open it looked worn and strained now that it was the near the end of the 1950s. Late one night, when the people were long asleep, Bridge struck up a conversation with Old Bridge.

"Will we always be side by side?" Bridge asked.

"No, I'm to be taken apart and sold for scrap iron when you are complete."

"Oh, I'm sorry."

"Don't be. I've had my day. Lots of people and trains have gone over me and thousands of ships have passed through when I was opened. Once, back in 1905, a huge ship named the *Northern Wave* hit my center span! What a wreck that was! Fortunately, only three people were on me at the time—the engineer and two pedestrians. None of them were killed. But it took a long time to repair me."

"I hope I never get hit," Bridge commented.

"Bound to happen sometime. I almost got hit again in 1940, but that ship's anchor held when they dropped it, and I was not damaged. Now, I'm just too narrow, old, outdated and ready for the scrap heap. It's okay; it happens to all things built by people."

All the pilings for three large oval "holes" had now been driven into the mud at the bottom of the lake. Bridge felt a tingling when the water was pumped out of those holes and sand poured in. Soon, there were "sand islands" where the base of Bridge would be. He listened to the construction workers of the American Bridge Company as they talked about the upcoming work. He was to be built using the "Caisson" method. Piers would be forced down through twenty-five feet of water, forty-five feet of mud and another five feet into the solid gravel below the lake bed.

Concrete would be poured into wedge-shaped molds, cutting down through the sand like giant cookie cutters. Their own weight would force them downward at the rate of three inches per hour, day and night. More concrete would be added to the top as needed. Once the wedges reached the gravel under the mud, the water would again be pumped out, the shafts sealed and highly-pressurized air would be forced in.

Bridge and Old Bridge talked each night about what they heard during the day. "That designer from Hazlet and Edral, the consulting engineers out of Chicago, was here again today," Bridge said.

"What did he have to say?"

"Pretty soon, some specialized workers will arrive. They have to be in the very best physical condition. I heard them called 'sand hogs.' They're specially trained to work under very high air pressure. I thought I heard them say the pressure is much greater than ordinary air, but I didn't catch all of it—pounds per square inch or some such thing. Anyway, it's very dangerous."

"I wasn't built that way," Old Bridge said.

"No, I guess things have changed a lot since you were built. These special men have to enter something called a compression tank for half an hour before they go to work digging out the last five feet of gravel. They can only work a couple hours at a time and then have to go into that compression tank again for half an hour before entering the regular air."

"Why?"

"Apparently, if they don't do the compression tank thing, they will get something people call 'the bends.' There's even an air lock for the bucket of gravel they dig up when it goes up to the surface! They will work in those short shifts, taking turns. These will form the three deep-water piers that will hold up my superstructure."

By the end of that process, 9,000 tons of steel-reinforced concrete would go down those holes. Also, there would be seven "regular" piers in shallower water built using coffer dams. The coffer dams were much like the "sand islands" built into deeper water, but once the steel pilings were in place, and the water pumped out, the concrete piers would be driven into the lake bed with more usual methods, rather than the compressed air chambers for those that went down fifty feet below the lake bottom.

Bridge soon understood that he would not be a swing bridge like the two before him. He had a truly unique design—a lift bridge like an elevator. His center span would rise up to let ships pass underneath and then be lowered again. This would be much faster to open and shut than the old swing bridge, which had taken up to half an hour to open for a ship to pass through and then another half hour to close. Bridge could lift in minutes by comparison, cutting down on the traffic backup. He would have four lanes—two each way—so many vehicles could go over him much more quickly. There would also be pedestrian lanes on each side. Like Old Bridge, he would have a railroad on the lower level, but he would have one more unique feature: the railroad level could be set in the middle so vehicles could drive on it as well as the road level. This would place Bridge thirty-two feet above the water for most pleasure boats to pass under without stopping vehicle traffic! The plan was to set Bridge at the middle level through the shipping season. That way, the bridge only needed to stop traffic for the largest ships to pass through when he was at his highest—100 feet above the water—or be placed at the lowest level at those times when a train needed to cross.

Bridge was especially proud of what he would become when, one day, he heard a man named Kris Mattila say he was, "the most significant civil engineering structure, exclusive of the mines, in the western Upper Peninsula." Bridge also heard people say that lift bridges needed to be something called "span heavy." The railroad was on the west side of the bridge, making it unbalanced, so the west side counter weight of his lifting mechanism would have to be heavier, as well. He would be the heaviest lift bridge built up to that time.

A whole new group of specialized workers arrived when they began to build Bridge's superstructure. Over 200 skilled trades were involved in Bridge's construction. He watched as the steel beams arrived during the winter. They were piled on the Hancock side of the lake. They had been fabricated "downstate" and arrived by rail. Construction moved out from both sides to the towers, where the controls for lifting and lowering would be. The center span began to come together on barges tied to the shore and would later be floated into position.

Up and up went the road sections and towers on each side, rivet by rivet, 240,000 of them, each of which had to be tested for strength. A 250-foot gap remained between the towers, waiting for Bridge's 4.5 million pound center span. It was an amazing and tense day when his center span floated into place. The span took up all but eight inches of that gap between the towers, four inches on each side. Hundreds of people turned out to watch. After a full day of preparation, the center span was ready on September 9, 1959. Tugs eased the barges away from the shore in an operation that took the full day. Skilled tug operators "threaded the needle" and guided the center span into the gap between the two towers.

Bridge, and all the workers and watchers, breathed a huge sigh of relief when the center span rested exactly where it was supposed to! Pulleys weighing sixty-five tons, giant chains and counter weights constructed of huge boxes filled with concrete were ready to hold the center span. All during the construction, a rescue boat had been ready to pick up any worker who accidentally fell into the cold lake. Bridge was glad that it was never needed.

Now, months of testing, inspecting, checking, lifting and lowering Bridge's center span, double checking and more double checking happened before traffic could be allowed to cross him. Finally, on December 20, 1959, even though he would not be fully complete until the next year, Bridge was ready! The shipping season was over for that year, so there would be no opening for ships, but vehicle traffic and trains now streamed across him every day.

The two bridges bid each other goodbye that night, and Bridge watched with a measure of sadness the next day as workers started to take Old Bridge apart.

Spring came and the ice broke up. Ships approached and passed through with ease. In early June, disaster almost struck (as Old Bridge had told Bridge was sure to happen) when the *J. F. Schoellkopf* almost collided with Bridge! The captain reversed his engines and dropped anchor. But the anchor tangled in two of six Michigan Bell Telephone lines on the bottom of the channel. The captain ran his ship aground in shallower water and avoided a direct collision, but 1000 people in Hancock lost their phone service for a few days.

On June 25, 1960, Bridge was formally dedicated. If he was not already puffed up with pride, the summer sun expanded him even more, all within the expansion cracks planned for him. Marching bands crossed with a troop column, tankers and fighters. Jets flew over. Important people cut ribbons and made speeches. People watched from wherever they could catch a glimpse along the roads leading to Bridge, along the shore and up and down the streets near him.

Bridge has seen and heard a lot since then—some good and some sad memories. There was a lovely summer night when a celebratory parade of pleasure boats went under his center span, all decorated with lights and streamers. There were prizes, and the first prize winner was a graceful sailboat. The family aboard had a portable generator on the bow with which they powered strings of Christmas lights up the mast and the wire cables that held the mast in place. Lights ran all along the deck as well—a giant Christmas tree. Then, there was the sad day in 1982 when the last train used his lower level to cross. Copper mining had ended and passenger trains no longer had enough paying people to stay in business. Then there was that day in the spring of 1983 when a power loss stalled him part way up, and it took an hour and a half before he could fully open for the ship that wanted to pass. And that same fall, when his span froze halfway up for something like seventeen minutes. The steamer wanting to come through successfully dropped anchor and waited.

On September 9, 1989, a man and woman were allowed to have their wedding ceremony on Bridge. He had never seen such a thing before and was fascinated. Unfortunately, a hydraulic line broke and left them stranded up there for a few hours. All in attendance were very good-natured about it.

Bridge's operators now keep him in his middle position most of the year, only lifting him for a few large ships, like the *Ranger III* on its twice-weekly trips to Isle Royale National Park, and sailboats with tall masts. When the lake freezes over, he is lowered so snowmobiles can cross him all winter on trails that often parallel regular roads. He's always extra happy when Bridge Fest happens in the summer and at other times when parades go from Hancock to Houghton or the reverse.

If you live in the Keweenaw, you already know where to find him. If you are a visitor to the area, following US 41 northbound, or M-26, and cross over him, you'll turn right to head toward Lake Linden, or left to drive through Hancock. There are plenty of places to get a good view along both the Houghton and Hancock shorelines. Stop for a while in Houghton at the Carnegie Museum of the Keweenaw: 105 Huron St., Houghton, Michigan, 49931. They are open Tuesdays and Thursdays from noon to 5pm and Saturdays from noon to 4pm during the summer months. While their wonderful exhibit on the history of the bridge, which was done for Bridge's 50th Anniversary, is no longer on display, something just as interesting will be there.

Visit www.SuperiorTapestry.com/sites for more info, including the official MDOT documentary video "Keweenaw Crossing: Michigan's Elevator Bridge"

Fig. 15-3: Portage Lake Lift Bridge in the "down" position

Bridge in the lowered position as would have been used to allow railroad traffic to pass unimpeded, but motor traffic would be stopped.

Fig. 15-4: Portage Lake Lift Bridge in the middle position

Bridge as seen on an early October day in 2020. It is in the middle position to allow most pleasure craft to pass under without stopping traffic.

Chapter 16 – The Lady Be Good

Fig. 16-1: Propeller from *The Lady Be Good*

Propeller in his final resting place in front of the Lake Linden Village Hall.

Propeller waited in a warehouse, with many others just like her. They would be among the last pieces placed onto a B-24 Liberator Bomber aircraft. It seemed as though every person who entered the warehouse had something to say about the incredible process that began here before the United States entered World War II and after the Japanese attack on Pearl Harbor. Propeller listened and put the pieces together over time. She had been manufactured not long before she sat in the warehouse and soon learned from people working there that Consolidated B-24 Liberator bombers were built in several locations: San Diego, California, Ft. Worth and Dallas, Texas and Tulsa, Oklahoma, but that most were assembled right here at Willow Run near Detroit.

Later, Propeller learned that the construction of the Willow Run Plant, between Ypsilanti and Belleville, Michigan, was in itself a tremendous achievement. Acres and acres of buildings, one of them called "the world's largest enclosed room," had been dedicated June 16, 1941. Foremen often discussed the many problems they had overcome. Assembling aircraft was much more complex than putting together automobiles, not to mention the size of this bomber. Engineers had to solve the problem of applying mass production techniques to huge machines, breaking down the plane into sections, breaking down the sections into smaller units, then assembling the giant cranes and other machines that would put all the sections and parts back together again.

Ford Motor Company had even built a school to teach many specialty jobs to the hundreds of workers needed. Even with that, there were difficulties. Propeller heard some employees complain that the plant was an hour's drive from Detroit. People often asked those around them where they lived, searching for those close by with whom they could share rides. Gasoline and tires for automobiles were rationed, so fueling up one car, and each person only driving his/her own car one day a week, helped.

Propeller noticed many women among the employees, who worked just as hard as the men. One day, she heard a curious conversation.

"Did you see the dirty look old man Ford gave us when he visited the plant last week?" one woman asked.

"Sure did," said her friend. "You know, the old man only consults with his son Edsel now that he's retired. I heard a bunch of ladies on the line say the old man hates the whole idea of women working."

"Well, he doesn't have much choice now, does he? What with all our husbands off training for combat."

The two women laughed in spite of the nervousness in their voices and then headed back to the assembly line.

Propeller and three others were added to each of four powerful engines as one of the last steps in assembly. She was amazed to see that the B-24's wingspan was six feet longer than the B-17 she replaced, and the plane was slightly longer, as well. Inspectors and workers swarmed over the final stage of assembly. Propeller heard someone say each plane had something like 1,225,000 parts. Each part had been inspected, checked again as it was attached to other parts and tested over and over. Everything had to be perfect. Many parts had special coatings so that they functioned properly in extreme cold of high altitude flying, the heat of deserts, humidity of the tropics and cold climates of Arctic regions. A B-24's total weight was 20 tons, and she could carry 8,000 pounds of bombs and fly a 3,000 mile range at a high cruise speed.

During the final assembly and testing, Propeller heard many nicknames for the aircraft she was a part of: "Flying Boxcar," "Spam Can in the Sky," "Banana Boat" and "Pregnant Cow." There was some talk around the airfield that trained military crews preferred the former B-17. There were whispered complaints that the plane didn't perform well at low speeds, but the general staff much preferred the new B-24 with its four super-charged radial engines and parts that were interchangeable due to the engineering of the mass assembly process.

Propeller learned that when this plant reached the height of production, the bosses expected some 650 aircraft to roll off the assembly line each month. She could feel the pride of every man and woman who had stamped out the aluminum sheeting of the aircraft's skin, joined two circuits together, attached a single bolt among thousands or made hundreds of rivets. Whether soldier or factory worker, everyone across the entire country played a role, small or large. And Propeller was proud to be part of it.

Once outside of the assembly plant, the bomber with Propeller was tested again by a ground crew going over every system of the plane. Then, a flight crew took over, entering through her bomb bay doors, revving up her engines, testing the radio, taxiing her onto a runway—Willow Run Air Field—built right on site. The excitement of that first rising from the ground, a radio check, testing each engine—turning one off, then back on, the next one off, then on, making sure the plane still flew without one, or even two engines. The test crew talked about how B-24s were built so that if one engine was destroyed by gunfire, they could still fly, although crews would have to shut down an engine on the other side to balance the craft. In that instance, the plane then flew much slower, and the crew needed to get it back to base as soon as possible.

A crewman in the gun turret fired fake bullets from the mounted machine guns; another tested the bomb bay doors and dropped dummy bombs. The fact that the B-24's bomb bay doors rolled up into the fuselage like the front of a roll top desk was just one more advantage to the complex engineering that had gone into this aircraft.

Test crew members made their way along her centerline ventral catwalk, a nine-inch-wide structural keel beam connecting the individual parts of the plane. It would always be tricky for crew members to move about in this way, but it was all part of the design that led to as little air drag as possible while keeping weight low.

The plane with Propeller would have a crew of nine, but she heard that other B-24s could, and often did, have ten-man crews. Pilot and copilot were in the nose and, behind them, sat the radio operator. Then, the navigator and the bombardier occupied the forward part of the aircraft as well. Sometimes, these crew members doubled as flight engineers and gunners, since this forward area had two defensive machine guns. The waist area of the plane would be occupied by the ball turret gunner. Propeller could see that remarkable piece of the plane, which was pulled upward during take-off and landing. And, finally, the tail gunner sat at the very back of the plane. Crew members never knew when they might have to take over for each other in an emergency.

From the plant and air field at Willow Run, it was a long journey for this particular aircraft with Propeller on it, and many just like it, to Wheelus Air Base in Libya, not far from the town of Benghazi.

There, Propeller heard the names of those assigned to her crew, all of them new, learning to work together and anticipating the bombing missions to come:

- First Lieutenant William J. Hutton, Pilot
- Second Lieutenant Robert F. Toner, Copilot
- Second Lieutenant D. P. Hays, Navigator
- Second Lieutenant John S. Woravka, Bombadier
- Technical Sergeant Harold J. Ripslinger, Flight Engineer
- Technical Sergeant Robert E. La Motte, Radio Operator, and a native of Lake Linden in Michigan's Upper Peninsula
- Staff Sergeant Guy G. Shelly, Gunner/Assistant Flight Engineer
- Staff Sergeant Vernon L. Moore, Gunner/Assistant Radio Operator
- Staff Sergeant Samuel E. Adams, Gunner

Together, these nine young men named their plane *Lady Be Good* and proudly hand-painted it on the nose of the aircraft. Other crews named their planes as well, sometimes painting colorful pictures on their craft, depending on the artistic talent of each group of men. Propeller's crew began to fly training missions around the air base so they could handle the plane, use all its equipment, become a little familiar with each other's jobs and work together as a team.

The *Lady Be Good*, including Propeller, was proud to be part of the 376th Heavy Bombardment Group when, at last, they were ready to fly combat bombing missions. Of course, Propeller and her attached engine made a terrific amount of noise in flight, so she could not hear the voices of the crew inside the aircraft, but she could sense what was going on through the various electrical circuits.

An excited, proud and nervous crew prepared for take-off somewhere around 0200 hours April 5th, 1943, as part of a large group of bombers intending to drop their load on Naples, Italy. *Lady Be Good* was the last bomber to take off that day and was significantly behind the rest of the group. While they tried to catch up, and Propeller, with the others, worked her hardest to spin faster, they never did reach their group.

She sensed their dilemma: go on alone or abort the mission and return to base?

Since they kept going, Propeller knew the crew had decided to continue on and try to complete the mission. Somewhere along the line, the plane's parts sensed that the crew hoped they were over the target area; the bomb bay doors opened and they dropped their load. Then the news went through the circuits that the automatic direction finder was not working. It only had a single loop antenna, with no way to identify return or opposite readings. Propeller was sure that the navigator was trying his best, but everyone and everything were now concerned for their safety.

The wires and circuits could hear radio operator Robert La Motte's calls for help, but no answers came. Bad luck led to worse, as a sand storm developed over the desert around their base. The flares lit up to help returning bombers see the runway were not visible. The *Lady Be Good* continued south. Fuel began to run low.

Confused by the darkness of night and lack of proper visibility once beyond the sand storm, the crew thought they were still over the Mediterranean Sea. The crew put on their Mae West life vests and prepared to bail. They carried as little equipment as possible and jumped out of the aircraft, now descending rapidly as the engines sputtered for lack of fuel.

"No one is flying us!" the *Lady Be Good* and all her carefully made and inspected parts shouted. *"What do we do?"*

Fumes and air currents carried the plane another sixteen miles south after the crew bailed before she met the desert in the Calanshio Sand Sea. Propeller bent upon impact, and the plane broke into two pieces that landed close together. Overall, the craft was relatively intact. What the crew thought were waves turned out to be sand dunes! Later, the circuits buzzed as the still-working radio crackled with the voices of the base radio operator, calling out again and again to the crew, who were not there to answer.

Propeller sat in the desert and waited as the wind covered her, and the *Lady Be Good*, with sand, uncovered her and covered her again...

Then, one day, Propeller heard something besides the wind— voices. People on an oil exploration team from British Petroleum were scouting the area for likely places to drill for black gold beneath the desert sand. Propeller watched them make a note of her location with the date: November 9, 1958. But they never came back. Finally, on May 26, 1959, a crew from Wheelus Air Base traveled several hundred miles to reach the wreck of the *Lady Be Good*.

They walked about the two pieces of the craft. One looked at Propeller and the name on the aircraft.

"Well, I'll be damned! The *Lady Be Good*! How the hell did it end up this far south?"

Another chimed in. "Look at this! Water and supplies! There's still tea in this thermos." A sniff and a small sip. "And it's still good!"

Then someone shouted, "Stand clear!" and tried the machine guns. Rat-a-tat-tat! Still operable! Another person tried the radio— and it worked.

"No sign of parachutes; they must have bailed."

Propeller heard them discuss how the air base had sent out search and rescue operations right after the crash all around the base, and out over the Mediterranean, looking for wreckage and survivors. They found nothing. After several days, the search was abandoned. It was assumed that the plane had gone down into the sea.

"And here she is, the 'Ghost Bomber'! We've found her. But what happened to the crew?"

The group of men stood in reverent silence. Then, they attended to the task of figuring out what to do with the wrecked aircraft now that part of the mystery was solved.

Propeller watched as another group set out from her location, in February of 1960, with the mission of trying to find the remains of the crew. Judging from the angle of impact, they estimated the flight path of the plane and set out north. Propeller could not see, of course, but she later heard that some sixteen miles north, they found parachute straps, boots and life vests, dropped along a northward trail and still lying in the sand, indicating the direction the crew had gone. On February 11, they found the remains of Hatton, Toner, Hays, La Motte and Adams about 200 miles north of the crash, but still 160 miles south of the base.

Shelly's and Riplsinger's bodies were found May 17, 1960. And finally, on August 2, they found Lieutenant Waravka. Moore's body was never recovered. People speculated that perhaps his parachute had not opened completely.

Once the wrecked plane and Propeller were salvaged and returned to the air base, Propeller heard people talking about how they found a diary in co-pilot Robert Toner's pocket, detailing the suffering of the crew on their journey north. None of them were aware that they were over land when they bailed. Locating each other with flares and gunshots, they gathered to decide what the best action might be. They had only one canteen of water among them. Guessing that they were perhaps 100 miles south of their base, they made the decision to walk north, leaving things behind as they went to lighten their loads and leave a possible trail for those who might search for them.

After eight agonizing days of heat, wind and sand, with only the tiniest sips of water and no food, five of them were too spent to go on. They waited together in the hope that the other three would return with help. The three, with some strength, plodded on and on. Ripslinger made it the farthest—another twenty-seven miles beyond where the others lay in the sand, dried skin on bone.

Propeller heard that the search party carefully prepared each body for transport back to their home towns. And as they did so, they may have speculated (with 20/20 hindsight) what else the crew might have done. Propeller had thought these same things over the years of sitting in the sand.

If they had only known how far south they had strayed...if they had walked south toward where the plane went down, they could have used the emergency supplies left on board...and the radio was there to get help...if they had only known where they were...

The wreckage of the *Lady Be Good* remained at Wheelus Air Base. A man named Octave DuTemple, another Lake Linden native, saw it while on an inspection tour in 1968. Remembering Robert La Motte, one of Lake Linden's fallen heroes, he asked if it would be possible to have one of the propellers shipped to La Motte's and his home town. His request was granted.

So, Propeller came to stand above the Honor Roll in front of the Lake Linden Village Hall, and in her own quiet way, honoring all those who fought in WWII from that town, the Upper Peninsula, the State of Michigan, the nation and those who lived, worked and banded together to mine the minerals used to build her, engineer her parts and workings and assemble her.

Lest we forget the Greatest Generation.

The propeller of the *Lady Be Good* may be seen in front of the Lake Linden Village Hall: 401 Calumet St., Lake Linden, Michigan 49945

If visiting during the summer months, be sure to stop in and view the displays at the Houghton County Historical Museum: 53102 M-26, Lake Linden, Michigan 49945. Call 906-296-4121 for hours and days, which vary because it's an all-volunteer group.

Visit www.SuperiorTapestry.com/sites for more info including a video tour of the historic Willow Run factory where B-24s many were built.

Fig. 16-2: B-24 in action

15th Air Force B-24s fly through flak and over the destruction created by preceding waves of bombers.

Chapter 17 – A Stone's Story

Fig. 17-1: the former St. Anne's Church

Caption: The former St. Anne's Church, now The Keweenaw Heritage Center, as seen from across 5th Street in front of a café.

Stone began over a billion years ago as sand eroded from an even earlier rock, part of a chain of ancient mountains, long after named the Huron Mountains. The sand flowed with the rain and rivers down and down until it settled on the shore of a lake much more ancient than Lake Superior. Waves rippled the sand. More sand washed over that, and over that, and over that. The only life existing on earth then consisted of colonies of Stromatolites, or blue green algae, which (through photosynthesis) slowly raised the level of oxygen in the air to a point where other life would evolve in time. Colonies of Cyanobacteria sometimes blocked the flow of water through the sand, so iron particles did not oxidize. This type of bacteria, non-green plant organisms with a dark blue color, grew in round colonies and left white spots in some of the red sands around what would become Stone. It had taken nearly half the planet's history to get to this point. Dinosaurs, still in the far distant future, would never leave a trace in this sand.

Layers and layers of sand washed upon each other, pressing down and down, thousands of feet thick. The sand that would become Stone felt the pressure of those layers squeezing individual particles of sand together until they fused into rock, a special type of sandstone that humans, eons later, would call Jacobsville sandstone. Stone was patient through all this, having gone from rock to sand, to a new kind of rock, enduring through it all. What else did he have to do? So, he remained in darkness, deep below Earth's surface, dimly aware of the flows of lava cooling into basalt, with some cracks opening up, which would fill with copper and other metals by volcanoes not so far from Stone.

The land above Stone changed over millions of years: oxygen levels rose and the planet warmed and teemed with life, death and new life. Millions and millions of years more, Stone waited. Time marched on. On four different occasions, glaciers—hundreds of feet thick—gouged and carved the rock on the surface, scouring out life in their advances, renewing life in their retreats, sculpting the land to their way of thinking, dragging some pieces of rock and metal hundreds of miles from where they were before, then leaving them behind on the surface. But Stone knew none of what occurred way above where he waited. Waited for what?

Only long afterward would Stone find out from other rocks around him that Earth circled the sun millions of times; species of life came and went. Very late in geologic time, human beings evolved, spread throughout the Earth and, during the last Ice Age, reached the area where Stone waited far below the surface. Stone didn't know these early people were there, hunting, gathering berries and wild rice, fishing and finding some of the red metal near the surface not all that far from him. They hammered the red metal into bowls and jewelry, traded it until some pieces reached far south on the continent. Centuries went by.

In the modern year of 1883, Stone began to hear strange noises—pounding, grinding, scraping. He wondered what these noises were as he lay in the dark, some feet in from a cliff edge and below the noises. Later, he would see that human beings had removed some fifty feet of glacial drift and shale from the surface, had cut channels into the face of the sandstone, drilled a series of holes and cracked out blocks eight feet, by four feet, by two feet. With steam-powered machines, they lifted the blocks onto tram cars, hauled them to a dock on the shore of Lake Superior and loaded the blocks onto ships. The quarry was an ant hill of human activity.

Closer and closer, louder and louder the noise came to Stone. One day, the light reached him. Wedges separated him from surrounding rock. What a different world it was from his last view of it as sand, water and sky—then, there were no green or moving, living things. Now, life was everywhere: creatures on two and four legs, birds, trees, grass. As men and machines removed Stone from the cliff, he heard voices.

"Where are these blocks headed?"

"Calumet—for the building of a church. They'll be pleased with these blocks for the front—not a speck of those strange white spots."

As Stone was loaded onto a tram car, he heard he would travel some eighteen miles, first by ship and then by rail, to a town called Red Jacket. He continued to listen to the voices around him and learned that other blocks of stone from this quarry had been shipped to places as far away as Chicago and New York for handsome buildings in those great cities. Hundreds of buildings, and a few of the most expensive homes in what he heard called "The Copper Country," had been built, and would continue to be built, from blocks cut from the cliff from which Stone came.

Once at the building site, he was again admired for his pure, red color. "Hey, Cap," he heard one man say, "This one would be great for the name stone above the door!"

Cap agreed. "Get the sculptor over here."

A man with a special chisel admired Stone and carved into his surface: Saint Anne's Church 1900.

Some of the side walls of the church contained sandstone that had white and red stripes, pieces with white spots in them and other features considered less perfect by the builders. But the entire front of the building was as Stone—solid red. Below, around and then above him, blocks were cut, shaped, fitted together with mortar, formed into Gothic arches, stairs and a towering spire. People passed by, admired the progress and awaited the day the church would be complete. Stone was proud to be part of it, especially being the part showing the building's name.

From the people walking by, admiring this grand addition to their community, he learned that this new church stood where an older building had been. Called St. Louis de France, it had grown too small for the 375 families worshiping there. The priest had inspired his congregation to raise $45,000, a huge sum in those days, for their new church. At its height, the parish would have over 900 members. Inside were not just one main altar, but two side altars, finely crafted panels and walls, stained glass windows that Stone would hear were the envy of other churches. Architects would copy some of the ideas for another church a few blocks away and even others in nearby towns.

On Sunday, June 18, 1901, there was a solemn and impressive parade, with several bands making beautiful music and thousands of people walking the entire length of Fifth Street in Red Jacket before coming to a stop in front of the church. The Bishop of Marquette was there as well as many priests of other parishes and people from all over. The church, in song and ceremony, was consecrated for its sacred purpose. If Stone could have, he would have radiated gold rays from himself, so happy was he to be part of all this. After all the eons in the dark, he was part of something filled with light and spirit. And it happened in a mere blink of time since he had formed.

For sixty-five golden years, Stone rejoiced as people entered every Sunday—so many there was more than one service held—to sing, pray and receive Holy Communion. On weekdays, there were fewer people, but they still came. Stone watched brides and grooms enter to be married and, over the years, baptize their babies, lay their parents to rest and watch their children marry, the cycle of faith and life going on and on. He loved the grand music of the organ and to hear the choir singing and chanting in the loft behind the wall he adorned. He enjoyed the echo of the French language being taught in the basement of the church.

But nothing ever stays the same. For nearly a year between July 1913 and April 1914, the copper miners and the mine owners quarreled violently over working conditions. Other area churches had several more than the usual number of funerals. The spire of St. Anne's spread the word that men marched in the street and fought with each other just a few blocks away. The following Easter brought calm, but no one seemed truly satisfied. For a few years, things were "normal" again, but Stone noticed that the number of people living in the area gradually declined. Fewer worshipers came on Sundays, then only one Mass was held and even fewer congregants. The spire reported that many people and families boarded the train and never came back. Some mines closed and businesses, too. The train stopped coming to the depot. Automobiles became the main mode of travel.

In half a blink of his life, the glow was gone. The organ fell silent. In 1966, St. Anne's was deconsecrated, no longer a sacred place. Stone would hear from the people passing by that St. Anne's was one of three churches closed that year. Remaining parishioners left and attended one of the other two Catholic churches in the Calumet area. People wept. If he could have, Stone would have cried, too.

For five years, the church sat empty. No one entered the great door below Stone. He sat patiently, as he had for a billion years, wondering what would come next. What came was disappointment.

"Did you hear?" a person said. "Some guy bought St. Anne's from the diocese for only $4,000! Plans to open an antique store." The person to whom she spoke shook her head. It was 1971 when the sign went up: Olde St. Anne's Antiques and Collectables.

Stone thought, *Well, at least I'll be used again.* But only $4,000? The stone had listened to the words of the priests all those years—Jesus, betrayed for a paltry thirty pieces of silver. Stone felt betrayed, too. The shop was basically a junk shop, an on-going garage sale, and a mess. Few people came in and even fewer bought things. The owner cared nothing for the building itself, doing not a speck of upkeep.

Stone cringed when, in 1991, a second-rate movie company used the "sanctuary" to film a scene of a horror movie, *Children of the Night.* Stone could not see inside, but he heard that the movie featured shots of the stained-glass windows reflected on a flooded interior. A beautiful place of reverence had been reduced to a place of horror. But the worst was yet to come.

The junk shop owner died, leaving the mess for his estate to clean up, with no electricity or water connected. Stone heard the interior parts of the building groan as plaster sagged in the choir loft, missing stair treads stood to trip any who entered, having to skirt broken boards and holes in the main floor. One woman who entered had to catch herself on her elbows when the floor gave way beneath her. Pigeons flew through the former sanctuary, entering through holes in the eves. The steeple swayed; sandstone blocks loosened. Feathers, bird waste, dead pigeons and junk from the "antique store" lay everywhere. Gone from the basement meeting room were the hardwood floors, the dirt floor beneath dug up. An eight-inch-thick tree with knobs of branches held up the floor of the chancel area. Some of the glass bricks in the basement windows broke and animals entered. Mold covered the walls. Small trees took root in the cracks of the front steps. Mortar fell out from between the stones.

Two people passed by the front. One of them said, "The estate people want to get rid of the mess. I heard they want to sell it to someone who only wants to take out the stained-glass windows."

"I heard that, too," said the other. "Removal of glass would create a wind tunnel. With the leaking roof, cracked glass blocks in the basement and that porous sandstone expanding and contracting, summer to winter... Look at all the cracks! The whole thing will just fall in."

If stones could weep, Stone would have. *Perhaps I shall be worn down to sand again. Be patient*, he reminded himself. *Perhaps in another billion or so years...*

But the pride of the community would not let that happen. People walking by said that in 1994, the Calumet Downtown Development Authority appealed to area churches for help. Stone heard that Rev. Bob Langseth alerted people to the situation and began a fundraising campaign to buy the building. A committee formed a board to raise the purchase price of $38,000. The Township would own the church and provide insurance, but some other organization would have to do all the restoration and future maintenance. The Village of Calumet and the Township had barely enough tax money to maintain basic services. Volunteers entered the old church for first time in many years, beholding the reality of the building's ruin.

"I can't believe you didn't just walk away from it," Stone heard someone say as they surveyed the disaster. But this community did not give up. They raised the purchase price and took the first steps to stabilize the structure. Stone began to have hope.

Mask-wearing volunteers scraped away old plaster from walls and sagging ceilings. The roof could not yet be replaced, but they patched the leaks. They threw the flea market junk down through a hole in the main floor where it piled up. Five, two-ton dump trucks carted away that junk, rotting lumber, dead animals and pigeons and their accumulated waste.

Three years later, a loose block of sandstone from the steeple crashed onto Fifth Street. Stone worried as this new crisis diverted funds from full repair to the roof. A grant from State of Michigan allowed improved heating pipes to the basement, restoration of tuck-pointing of mortar between the blocks of sandstone. But the stained-glass windows were in danger of collapse. Michigan granted another $75,000, and people of the surrounding communities raised another $87,000 in donations to save the windows. Some were repaired on-site, while others were carefully removed and shipped to Philadelphia to Willett Studios, where specialists worked on them throughout the year 2000. Stone began to have hope.

That was a turning point, 100 years after building of the church. Seven years after the resurrection work began, the roof was finally completed. One of the board members said, "Well, old girl, you're going to stand."

Stone wanted to shout for joy.

The following June, the board, eager to have people see their efforts, raise more needed funds and promote the use of the building for local events, celebrated 100 years with a banquet in the basement meeting hall. They served elegant hors d'oeuvres in a place with one working toilet. The church was a mere shadow of its former self, but hints of its beauty were everywhere. The event's main speaker quoted Emerson: "'If eyes were made for seeing, then beauty is its own excuse for being.' People ask why we want to continue. My answer is, 'It's a beautiful building. It deserves to live.'"

A new sign went up on the front: *Keweenaw Heritage Center*

Where the altar once stood, now lies a stage with a line of flags along the back wall. On the far left, Quebec's provincial flag stands to honor the French-Canadian congregation who built St. Anne's.

The United States flag stands on the far right. Between them, in alphabetical order, are the flags of the countries from which people immigrated to the area in the early 20th century. These are also symbolic of their descendants, who rolled up their sleeves to renew the building and preserve their history.

Every summer, a new historical exhibit lines the walls of the former sanctuary. Chairs in rows welcome people to listen to concerts by local musicians. A basket passed at each concert collects donations for ongoing restoration.

In 2007, the first wedding took place, with a reception downstairs following the ceremony. The building also hosted a traveling exhibit from the Smithsonian and ethnic group meetings in fall and spring. The board began finding funds to restore an antique Barckhoff organ to be placed in the choir loft. It was not the original organ, but it was built around the same time. Volunteers dismantled it and carried it – piece-by-piece from the main floor to the choir loft. They accomplished this through an "Adopt-a-Pipe" fundraiser. The following year, the timber floor was refinished, sanded and varnished. Stone rejoiced when organ music once again echoed through the building.

A caring community continued to pour money and time into the Keweenaw Heritage Center. In 2008, a "Lift the Lift" campaign was funded by donations and a grant from the Keweenaw National Historical Park. Soon, people with disabilities could enter the building from a back door on Temple Street and go up to the main floor or down to the banquet room.

Stone shook in fear when lightning struck the steeple in 2013 (the second time such a thing had occurred). Heavy rain put out the resulting fire, but there was still damage. People poured out into the streets, cleaning up shingles and wood that fell, putting plastic tarps over the damaged area to keep out the rain, donating money for the repairs.

The Keweenaw Heritage Center Board reported to the community that, over the years, people donated over 80,000 hours of work and in excess of $1.5 million with day-to-day maintenance and utilities, and more projects to come. Of that money, 53% came from private donations of mostly local residents in an economically depressed area. The other 47% came from grants. All these things Stone heard people discuss as he looked down over the main door.

Was it only one woman's imagination when she thought she saw tears of joy dripping slowly from Stone on a recent sunny, summer day?

Anyone may see this beautiful building, located at the head of Fifth Street in Calumet, Michigan, 49913.

Visit www.SuperiorTapestry.com/sites for more info.

Chapter 18 – At the Corner of 7th and Elm

Fig. 18-1: *Societa Italiana di Mutua Beneficenza*

Previous page: The last building to stand at the corner of 7th and Elm as seen on December 26, 2013. The flag is at half-mast due to the Christmas Eve disaster. Photo used courtesy of Michigan Technological University Archives and Copper Country Historical Collections, Nara Collection.

A short walk from the Keweenaw Heritage Center, the land at the corner of 7th and Elm Streets in Calumet has seen three different buildings come and go, all of them the property of the Italian Mutual Benefit Society. Street Corner witnessed many good things over the years. Yet, she is known for only one thing: Christmas Eve, 1913. She feels it is high time people knew there is much more to her history than that one tragic night.

The *Societa Italiana di Mutua Beneficenza* (Italian Mutual Benefit Society) was the first Italian organization in the Copper Country. Street Corner watched the organization grow to eighty-five members by 1875. Its main purpose was to help its members in times of emergency—an early form of life insurance and similar benefits. The society provided money to the families of members in cases of serious illness, accident or death. It was a male-only club, which might seem strange today, but Street Corner hopes you realize that the roles of men and women have changed greatly since the copper boom days. The area's prosperity depended mainly upon the copper mining industry, which was filled with danger, both underground and above, although the worst accidents were usually underground. In the years before workmen's compensation laws existed (and the earliest of such laws paid very poorly even by that day's standards), this type of help was much needed and appreciated.

Street Corner watched as the organization began to build its first building, a timber frame structure. The society planned to have regular membership meetings there, as well as a bit of income from renting the space to other groups for their meetings. The building was nearly complete in 1880 when a terrible wind storm blew it down. Street Corner seemed to sink the tiniest bit in sorrow and thought, *What will this group do now?* She should not have worried. Undaunted, the membership cleaned up the mess and began to build again.

The next building was also timber frame.

It had two stories, with the lower level rented out to retail stores. The upper level included a sizable hall for the organization's use and was, indeed, a fine space for other groups to rent for their meetings and events. Street Corner had learned from people's discussions around her that across the Copper Country, nearly every ethnic group had some sort of organization to help its members and to preserve their culture. The Germans had their group; the Irish of Hancock had the Ancient Order of Hibernians; there was a Swedish Benevolent Society; the Hungarians had no less than five such groups; there was a Finnish Benevolent Society, a Finnish Accident and Aid Association, and many more. Some of these were religious in nature, others secular or political, in addition to offering some sort of insurance benefits. Still others endeavored to preserve their culture at a time when grown children of immigrants were quick to "Americanize."

Street Corner, and the buildings around her, listened to heated arguments on many issues during some meetings. At one meeting, the action items on the agenda included collecting a fine from a member who had not attended a fellow member's funeral—a strict requirement of membership. The member argued that he had a valid reason for not being there. Some members supported him in this, but in the end, the member apologized and paid his fine. Other times, Street Corner saw the tears of a widow who gratefully accepted the money given her by the society to help her and her orphaned children survive after the death of the family's breadwinner. She also heard and enjoyed the thanks of families whenever a member's wife had ministered to another family in time of illness, bringing food or caring for children when a mother was too ill to do so—good Christian charity at its finest. Each ethnic group took care of its own, since they shared a language and some members spoke no other.

Street Corner also saw a lot of general merry-making when members and their families gathered to celebrate just about anything. Many groups believed beer and wine made the party better, but there were others who didn't drink any alcohol. Oh yes, Street Corner could tell you some tales, but she doesn't care to gossip.

On New Year's Eve 1907, a particularly jolly group rented the Italian Hall for a rip-roaring party. Street Corner listened as the party grew ever louder and the beer flowed. Everyone had a splendid time. After they all went home, a fire broke out in the kitchen. The whole building went up in flames!

Street Corner watched in horror, but could do nothing but wait for the volunteer firefighters to arrive. Water from fighting the fire, and snow melted in the heat, gushed along the street, washing over her curb. The Italian Society did not blame anyone—an accident was an accident—sometimes these things happened. On January 1, 1908, their building was nothing but a charred, black mess covered in dirty ice, the water having frozen again in the winter chill.

Street Corner rejoiced when the Italian Mutual Benefit Society decided to rebuild quickly—bigger and better. She listened closely to the architect they chose, who designed a building of brick and decorative Jacobsville sandstone in a style called Romanesque Revival, very popular in the mid-19th century. This style had been inspired by an earlier era in the 11th and 12th centuries featuring elaborate Roman arches, but the Romanesque Revival style was simpler than that of the previous time. Arches embellished the tops of seven windows on the second story. The main entrance leading to the second story had a larger, graceful arch and a vestibule that opened to both the adjoining retail space and a stairway about five feet wide, leading to the second floor.

The new building measured 58-by-110 feet. The roof support had "I" beams that sloped from the front to the rear. Tin ceiling tiles with decorative designs would adorn the second-floor meeting hall, which was 78-by-38 feet and included a raised stage area with a kitchen below the stage and an upper gallery looking down on the main hall. There was also a hallway with ticket windows and restrooms, a bar room and a fire escape from a vestibule between the restrooms and the bar room. The first floor consisted of space for two businesses with living areas behind the store fronts. There was also a basement, with each store having half the basement for storage.

The new building was dedicated on Columbus Day in October 1908. James McNaughton, general manager of the Calumet and Hecla Mining Company, wrote the dedication speech, but due to a death in his family, another person, Street Corner forgot who, read his words. *This is a fine day, indeed*, she thought.

Street Corner felt that the best time of her life was during this period, when the two storefronts were occupied by the Great Atlantic and Pacific Tea Company and Dominic Vairo's Saloon. She watched all day as customers—mainly women—went in and out of the A&P. In the evening, the men-folk took over with cheerful goings-on in the saloon. It was a daily parade of people, some in the elegant fashions of the day, others in the simpler clothes of working folk. The community as a whole was doing well—plenty of good jobs for families and single men, wealthy people and those who knew that, with hard work, they would also prosper. Many groups entered the Italian Hall for their meetings and events. Street Corner felt she was lifted up by everything around her in every season of the year.

Then came that infamous year of 1913, when everything changed.

Street Corner did not understand much about the events of that year and the violent labor strike against the mining companies. She only knew it changed her life and the lives of thousands of people forever—a horrid stain in history. Many meetings within the building echoed with angry voices; people marched every day in the streets, often fighting with each other. National Guard troops came to try to lessen the violence and keep the peace. Oh, it was truly terrible!

What began as a party for the families of the men on strike on Christmas Eve turned into tragedy when someone—nobody knew who, not even Street Corner—shouted *Fire! Fire!* It was a false alarm. Seventy-four people, sixty of them children aged two to sixteen, tried to flee the building and died in the crush of bodies on the stairs. The screaming, yelling and panicked chaos haunted Street Corner to the point that she has tried very hard to forget that night, along with the blame and accusations that followed.

The strike and its violence ended in the spring of 1914. Meetings and events continued for the Italian Mutual Beneficial Society, but it was never the same. The region entered a long, slow decline. Society membership dropped. The organization tried to counteract by having more family social and cultural gatherings, but it didn't help. By 1922, several Copper Country Italian groups combined to form the Christopher Columbus Society. Street Corner grieved as they used the Italian Hall less and less. The A&P and saloon owners couldn't seem to keep business coming their way and closed. No other businesses rented the spaces. In the Great Depression of the 1930s, there was less money than ever for the upkeep of the building.

As the years went by, the cornice deteriorated, had to be removed from the southernmost window and was boarded up. Street Corner became more hopeful when, on June 6, 1977, the State of Michigan declared the building a Historic Site. More hope came in July 1980, when the building was named to the National Register of Historic Places. But these honors did not provide the money needed for building maintenance and repair, as Helen Smith, owner at the time, hoped they would. She did not have the thousands of dollars needed for complete restoration. One estimate was close to $500,000, Street Corner heard.

Street Corner wanted to sink into the dark ground below her when the wrecking ball crashed into that fine building in October 1984. The earth shook beneath her with each crash of the ball. Was it the end of the world? At the least, it was the end of her world. Removal from those state and national historic registers naturally followed. Street Corner wasn't the only one bothered by the loss of dignity and self-respect with which she lived every day. Finally, a group of citizens, who cared about their community's history, reconstructed the distinctive arch from the doorway and built a memorial park to remember those who died on December 24, 1913. Street Corner knows that was the proper and civic-minded thing to do, and she admires their effort, but still, nothing in that park tells of the many good times or the charitable work of the *Societa Italiana di Mutua Beneficenza* or the other similar organizations of that period and the important resources they provided for their communities. While her spirits are somewhat brightened by the park, she hopes that more people will learn the rest of the story about the building that once sat upon her.

The memorial park is now owned by the Village of Calumet and maintained by the Keweenaw National Historical Park. You can visit any time. When you come to pay tribute to the tragedy of December 24, 1913, Street Corner would appreciate it if you spent a few minutes to remember all the good things that happened on that corner, too. Please visit www.SuperiorTapestr.com/sites for more info including a video documentary by Steve Lehto.

Fig. 18-2: Memorial Park monument

The Memorial Park over which the Corner of 7th and Elm Streets presides today

Chapter 19 – Piles of Poor Rock

Fig. 19-1: A Pile of Poor Rock

The spire of Bethany Lutheran Church, between the trees on the left, provides some perspective as to the size of this particular pile of poor rock in Mohawk, Michigan.

Mother Magma was an underground ocean of semi-liquid rock. Around 1.2 billion years ago, she regularly oozed out daughters who were sisters to each other—rivers of lava that slowly cooled into basalt, a gray volcanic rock. She did this in a way similar to a queen bee laying thousands of eggs that hatch into infertile female worker bees. Rising gas bubbles in each Basalt Sister formed rounded holes or almond shaped vesicles, pipe vesicles (long empty tubes) and other formations that filled with copper, smidgeons of silver and other trace minerals. These layers of the Basalt Sisters were then pressed down in the middle so that their "heads" bent upward to form the heights and ridges of the Keweenaw Peninsula, while the tips of some "toes" formed Isle Royale. Layers of sedimentary rocks were laid down among batches of the Basalt Sisters during times when Mother Magma went to sleep for a while. Faults at about a forty-five-degree angle at each end were named the Isle Royale Fault and the Keweenaw Fault. Later, many people would see not a number of "heads" but a "spine" of copper rich rock extending from Copper Harbor to Ontonagon. The toes on Isle Royale didn't yield much copper—not that people, ancient and modern, didn't try to make a profit there.

Some of the larger pipe vesicles full of native copper ended up on the surface due to erosion. Then, four rounds of glaciers scraped off parts of them, dragging them from one place to another and dropping them on the surface as "float copper." Over the eons, many of the Basalt Sisters eroded into layers of pebbles, rocks and sand, which were then pressed down and cemented together into another type of rock called conglomerate—with tiny bits of copper speckled throughout. These were then covered with more layers of new Basalt Sisters whenever Mother Magma decided to push more daughters out onto the surface, starting the whole process over again—layers of gray basalt, erosion, compaction, conglomeration, more basalt... for millions of years.

Human beings dug down, down and down into many of these Basalt Sisters. Several small mining companies failed. Huge ones, like Quincy and Calumet & Hecla, dominated the business scene from the 1860s well into the 1900s. The collective Basalt Sisters found themselves blasted apart, pounded into pieces of rock small enough for a man to lift and dump into a tram car, pushed down mine tunnels, dumped into a skip car and hauled to the surface. There, they were sorted. Pieces with enough copper were hauled to one place and those judged by humans to be "poor rock" were dumped elsewhere and everywhere.

Sisters with copper were further crushed into sand and heated so the copper floated to the top to be processed into copper ingots. Basalt sands found themselves dumped into Torch Lake, Portage

Lake and the shores of Lake Superior near Gay on the east side of the Keweenaw Peninsula and Frieda on the western shore, among other places. There, the sisters lay in a million, billion pieces of themselves, hoping to be reunited into some type of sedimentary rock in another billion years.

Piles of Basalt Sisters lay all over the Keweenaw: at the Clifton, Delaware and Central Locations, in Mohawk and Fulton, around the Calumet area, on down to Houghton and Hancock, then on to the Range Towns... scattered, left to sit in mounds like so much garbage. While some mines had higher percentages of copper than others, the poundage of waste rock went something like this: for every ton of rock that came out of the mines (2240 pounds equals one ton), about forty-nine pounds was copper and the rest "poor rock." At Calumet and Hecla (C&H), the highest percent copper ore came from the upper levels of their many shafts. But the average yield was forty-nine pounds per ton, times hundreds of tons per year, for seventy-three years. By only 1882, C&H had pulled an amount equal to 120 acres—who knows how deep—of poor rock! And the value of copper to that point equaled a staggering $71,200,000 [Statistics courtesy of Jeremiah Mason of the Keweenaw National Historical Park].

The Quincy Mine in Hancock went down over one mile into the earth, and it never really hit the "bottom" of layers of the Basalt Sisters. Imagine the amount of rock there, the number of Basalt Sisters run through with the main shaft, drifts and stopes on so many levels. To the human mind, the extent of the Basalt Sisters seems as unimaginable as travel to the far side of the Milky Way. The Sisters might have given all that information a "ho, hum."

What to do with all that rock?

While some people thought the Basalt Sisters were nothing but ugly gray garbage, others found creative ways to use them in construction, building truly beautiful buildings around the Copper Country. The Basalt Sisters liked being used that way, but sometimes they couldn't understand why people would find it difficult to tell the difference between them and Jacobsville sandstone. One Sister thought perhaps people were color blind and unable to see her lovely, solid gray composition compared to the red of sandstone or the pink and white stripes of Jacobsville's variations.

In 1887, a truly creative architect mixed pieces of one Basalt Sister into a complicated and lovely jigsaw puzzle to form the C&H office building at the corner of Red Jacket Road and US Highway 41. It replaced an earlier timber frame building on Mine Street. The builders, according to the architect's plan, used local poor rock, fieldstone, brick and sandstone trim to create a unique building. Additions, carefully matched to look the same, were completed in 1899, 1900 and 1909. During her life with C&H, Basalt housed local management—the corporate office was in Boston, Massachusetts. Upper-level management, the agent or superintendent, general manager, clerks and paymasters all had offices there. The building also held a drafting room, pay office, head mining engineer, a dark room, printing operation, other managers and stenographers. The pieces of Basalt in that grand building were proud to be part of a very different whole, with more pieces of her going into the company library across Red Jacket Road.

Fig. 19-2: Keeweenaw National Historical Park Headquarters

The former C&H office building on Red Jacket Road now houses the Keweenaw National Historical Park Headquarters.

Basalt often listened to meetings within the walls of the C&H building. Some were boring; some productive; some angry—like those during the copper strike in 1913. Decades later, there were somber meetings about how to keep the company going.

What will become of me now? Basalt thought when C&H closed down in 1968. Some staff remained into the early 1970s, but finally, the building stood vacant. Forlorn Basalt in the company office building looked across the street to the library and cried at their emptiness. The library had ended up with the Lake Superior Land Company. Other buildings were torn down—piles of garbage once again. Then, a group of physicians took over the building, remodeling it into suites of offices, labs, procedure rooms, restrooms and breakrooms. While not in sync with the historical nature of the building, at least Basalt was still in use. She was saddened, however, that inside her, the original wainscoting, trim, doors, wood floors, box beam ceilings, fireplaces and other lovely features were removed, covered with drywall, carpet, acoustic tile and dropped ceilings.

Her depression lifted when people of the area showed their respect by pushing for the creation of the Keweenaw National Historical Park in 1992 as a way to preserve the area's rich history. The park rented offices on the second floor, but when the doctors' group moved out in 1999 for a better place of its own, the Park Service made plans for major renovation and rehabilitation. The building stands there today, holding park offices, the interpretation and education division, historic preservation division, meeting and training spaces in a design as close to the original as possible. Other pieces of the Basalt Sisters had spread themselves around the Copper Country in the form of basement walls, for homes and buildings, and other C&H buildings up and down Mine Street. Those pieces of the Basalt Sisters that became part the foundations of various homes watched families move in, have children and then grow old together. They watched as housewives made countless trips down and up basement steps with arms full of home canned vegetables and apples, or baskets of laundry. Several generations and different occupants of each home paraded by those pieces of the Basalt Sisters, never giving them much thought, except when water from melting snow each spring seeped through cracks.

Fig. 19-3: Poor rock as a foundation element

Poor rock forms the foundation/basement of one of many such homes built
in the early 1900s

Other pieces of the Sisters became gravel for roads and driveways.
Any piece, large or small, of gray rock throughout the Copper
Country, is a piece of the Basalt Sisters. They'll be happy if you take
a scavenger trip around the area and see how many you can spot.

The parts of the Basalt Sisters ground into sand and dumped into
lakes did not get as fair a shake. As the mines ran deeper into the
ground, raising the cost of production almost above the market value
of copper, smelting technology improved. Companies found they
could mine their own sands dumped into Portage and Torch Lakes.
Mining managers decided to dredge the sand from one place, smelt it
again with better techniques to get more copper out of it and then
dump the waste back into another part of the same lake. These sands
contained tiny particles of lead, uranium and other heavy metals that
came along with the Basalt-Copper package, but not in quantities
enough to mine. These unwanted particles leached into lake waters
and ground water. Such dissolved minerals later seeped into

community water supplies and private wells. On windy days, sand blew into the towns of Lake Linden, Hubbell, Tamarack, Houghton and Hancock to annoy housewives. This dust also made its way into people's lungs.

During the 1980s and 90s, billions of Super Fund Cleanup dollars were used to cover these sand banks with a layer of topsoil and then planted with buffalo grass. Better grasses and bushes followed, as dead and rotting buffalo grass added to the topsoil. Today, most people would never know the sand banks filled so much of Torch Lake along the shore where C&H, Tamarack Mills and even Quincy dumped them. But the bottom of the lake knows. And some rather strange-looking fish have been caught there from time to time. This toxic mess probably contributed to a higher-than-average cancer rate for area residents. The Basalt Sisters are sorry about that, but then, it wasn't their fault.

The Basalt Sisters' sand from the Gay Stamp Mill decided to go wandering along the shore with the current of Lake Superior. They migrated all the way from Gay along several miles of shoreline to flow over the breakwater at Grand Traverse Safety Harbor, so that the channel had to be dredged out again—another costly affair, and a process not yet finished as of this writing. Parts of those Basalt Sisters also threaten Buffalo Reef, an underwater shoal area off the shore of Grand Traverse, which is critical habitat to spawning lake trout. Oh, those sisters were not very nice. But could they really help it? Who is to say?

You can't miss seeing pieces of the Basalt Sisters on a trip through the Keweenaw. They are everywhere. Dig through some of the piles. Perhaps you'll be lucky to find a piece with a bit of green oxidized copper in it for a souvenir.

And be sure to visit the Visitor Center displays on 5th Street and the Keweenaw National Historical Park Headquarters, 25970 Red Jacket Road, Calumet, Michigan, 49913 phone: 906-337-3168. Visit www.SuperiorTapestry.com/sites for more info including a video tour of the stamp sands at Gay.

Fig. 19-4: Migrating sands at Grand Traverse Bay

This view of the migrating sands along the breakwater of the Grand
Traverse Bay Safe Harbor shows some of the damage done by moving sand
and the work to remove it. The photo was taken in the summer of 2020.

Chapter 20 – Chrysler Calamity on the *City of Bangor*

Fig. 20-1: A 1927 Chrysler from the *City of Bangor*

Car as he looks today at the Eagle Harbor Lighthouse Museum.

Brand new, Car, a 1927 Chrysler, waited patiently in line to be loaded onto the *City of Bangor*,- or at least as patiently as any young car could. He'd rolled off the assembly line only a few days before, along with 219 other new cars just like him. Car was eager to reach an owner waiting for him in Duluth, Minnesota. The parking lot full of them moved slowly, a few driven at a time, closer to the crane loading vehicles into the hold of the ship.

Fig. 20-2: City of Bangor

Car found the ship an amazing thing—but he hadn't seen much in the first week or so of his life, so he found everything amazing. He knew from conversations around him that the *City of Bangor* was 372 feet long and forty-four feet wide with a draft of about twenty-three feet, and that it had been built in Bay City, Michigan in 1896. Car felt very confident in the ship and was excited to be loaded aboard. It was hard for him to be stuck near the end of the line.

A deck hand yelled from the ship as Car finally neared the front of the line: "Hold is full!"

A groan of, "NOOOOOO," came from Car's front grill, but of course, people could not hear him. "I can't be left behind now!"

Another shout came from men on the loading dock. "Boss says to lash the rest down on the top of the deck. He wants these new models to get there this year! Brand new!"

Thus it was that Car, and several of his brothers, were lifted onto the deck of *City of Bangor* and securely tied down. Car, over his fear of being left behind, now counted himself lucky to be able to see what was going on the entire trip. A cold, late November wind blew over the deck as the ship steamed up Lake Huron toward the locks at Sault Ste. Marie.

"Late in the season to be starting this run," Car heard a deckhand say.

"Yes, but the weather's been exceptionally good this November. We'll be fine."

"I don't know," the first deck hand continued. "Lake Superior can get pretty wild in late November."

"Bah, we can handle it. I've been on the Big Lake in November before."

Sure enough, as they went north on Lake Huron, the weather did clear some, and while it wasn't warm by any means, the sun was out. Car watched the ship's progress with awe. The shore streamed by quite a distance away. Waves sloshed up against the hull of *City of Bangor* and flowed along its side into the wake behind. Darkness fell and the stars sparkled overhead.

By morning, they approached the lower portion of Saint Mary's River. The ship slowed and all hands came on deck to prepare it to go through the lock at Sault Ste. Marie. *City of Bangor* glided slowly into the Sabin Lock, the newest at that time. Crew members threw ropes to lock hands standing above them on the sides of the lock. The gate behind the ship closed. Water began to swirl in, lifting the great ship gently. The crew on the ship and the lock hands took in the lines as the ship slowly rose twenty feet. Car hardly knew where to look next, so great was his amazement at what was happening. The gate ahead of the ship opened slowly. Lock hands tossed the ropes back to deck hands, who now stood above them. Deck hands and lock hands waved and shouted goodbye. *City of Bangor* steamed slowly out of the lock and on up the St. Mary's River into Whitefish Bay on the greatest of the great lakes, Lake Superior.

Once they cleared Whitefish Point, the captain set a straight course toward the tip of the Keweenaw Peninsula. Car watched the land grow smaller and smaller behind the ship until it disappeared into the horizon. All he could see was water everywhere. He felt like a speck on that inland, fresh-water sea. He heard a deckhand say that once they passed Manitou Island and cleared the point of the Keweenaw, they would set another straight course to a place in the middle of the western part of the lake, where they would make a slight angle to head southwest into Duluth. Yes, they would make it just fine and head back quickly to finish this run—right at the end of the shipping season.

Lake Superior, however, did not like their over-confidence. She kicked up one of her November gales as they approached Manitou, and once they rounded the point of the Keweenaw, they faced her full fury! Heavy snow blew almost horizontally. The *City of Bangor* wallowed in twenty-five-foot wave troughs, struggling to rise to the next crest. Car screamed in fright. The ship's crew and captain struggled to keep control as they slowly passed Copper Harbor—a place much too small for this ship to find safety—and a tricky one to enter, with rocky shoals on both sides of the channel. Halfway to Eagle Harbor, also much too small for this ship, the captain decided they must turn back and anchor on the lee side of Keweenaw Point and wait there until the storm ended.

They never made it.

Car wailed in terror as a huge wave swept eighteen of his brothers from the deck of the ship! Luckily for Car, he was close to the back of the ship and the "aft castle" (the tall area at the back of a ship where the wheel house and crew quarters are). That offered some protection. A little beyond tiny Horseshoe Harbor, and only two miles from their goal of safety on the other side of the point, the ship ran aground on the rocky shore.

There, the *City of Bangor* sat, wedged into a reef of sharp rock, quite close to shore. The crew scrambled down the lee, or protected, side of the ship and over a slab of ice to launch the life boats into a narrow gap of open water between them and the shore. All twenty-four crew members and the captain made it safely to land, but they had no food or medical supplies. It happened that Captain Tony Glaza, of the life-saving station at Eagle Harbor, was returning from a rescue on the other side of the Keweenaw near Point Isabelle. He saw the crew moving about on the shore. They saw him, too, and were certain that he would return to rescue them. Later, Car learned that Captain Glaza intended to do just that, as soon as he got back to Eagle Harbor to drop off the other unfortunates he had on board. That was around 3:30pm.

Car watched as the crew built a fire on shore to try to stay warm through the night and the raging storm. *Will they get us off, too?* he wondered. Snow, mixed with freezing rain, soon covered Car and his remaining brothers. Those below in the hold called up that they were all right where they were. The ship soon resembled an ice castle.

No help had come to the hungry, freezing crew by morning. Car found out later that the crew members knew it was only six miles to Copper Harbor and warm homes there, but it would be the longest six miles of their lives. Car watched in great anxiety as they began trudging through the snow. Car could not know the next part of the story, since he had to remain where he was, tied down and frozen onto the deck. He heard about it later.

Poorly clad for such a hike, crew members struggled for many hours while their equally cold officers urged them on, one step at a time. They arrived with frost-bitten feet at Fred the Swede's place in Copper Harbor. He had not room enough for all of them, so with help from Billy Bergh, he took them all by sleigh (a few at a time) to Bergh's house, where Mrs. Bergh—in spite of being short on supplies herself—warmed them and fed them for several days before Captain Glaza was able to return them to Calumet—by sleigh, not by boat.

It was mid-December before Car saw any more people. The bit of open water between the ship and the shore had long since turned to solid ice. Many men boarded the ship. They chopped Car and his brothers on deck free of their ice prison and, with ropes and capstans, began to maneuver Car and all the others off the ship, then to the shore and along a poorly-plowed roadway, to Copper Harbor where they were lined up at Charlie Maki's house. There, they sat again until men could plow a road to Copper Harbor from Phoenix and round up enough drivers to take the cars back to the railroad at Calumet. The caravan of new cars passed between snowbanks eight to ten feet high on each side of the road. Car was just glad his engine still worked. He wondered how he would reach Duluth and the owner who awaited him there.

Car didn't know it until much later, but the other cars never made it to Duluth. By the beginning of April, 1928, Car was one of two or three who had not yet been loaded onto railroad flat cars for a long ride back to Detroit. Those vehicles would go south through Wisconsin to Chicago and then on to Detroit, because there was no bridge across the Straights of Mackinac then. They would be cleaned up and sold at a discount because they were now "last year's" model and had been through a wreck. Their original prices had been from $780.00 to $830.00.

Car ended up staying behind. He went from one local owner to another over the years, appearing from time to time in parades on the 4th of July. That part of his life was quite enjoyable, because people cheered and clapped as his driver went slowly by them. At one point, Car heard one owner say that in 1932, Chrysler Company had a fire in their office building and records with vehicle identification numbers for many years were lost. No one could be certain that Car was part of the group on the *City of Bangor,* so his value as such was less. But he still has a small scar on one door where an axe had hit him as men chopped him out of the ice. He can't exactly remember how he ended up in a garage adopted to be part of a museum, but he likes it when people admire him. He is surrounded by photos and informational posters about him and his brothers' ordeal aboard the wreck of the *City of Bangor*. He has heard stories about how the ship was salvaged for the iron it was made of during World War II. One small piece of iron sitting by the wall near Car at the museum is all that remains of the ship.

You can visit Car at the Eagle Harbor Lighthouse Museum, 670 Lighthouse Road, Eagle Harbor, Michigan, 49950. It is open in June, September and October from 12 p.m. to 5 p.m., and during July and August from 10 a.m. to 5 p.m., seven days a week. Visit www.SuperiorTapestry.com/sites for more info.

Chapter 21 – A Tree's Tale

Fig. 21-1: Estivant Pines Sanctuary

Looking up into the heights of hundreds-of-years-old trees in the Estivant Pines Sanctuary fills everyone with awe.

Tree's life as a tiny seedling was a struggle for survival. Taller trees around her seemed to suck up all the sunlight, but Tree stretched upward and claimed her place among the other white pines on the hillside near the tip of the Keweenaw Peninsula. Hundreds of years later, people would note by her growth rings that she sprouted between Columbus' third and fourth voyages to the Caribbean. By the time Shakespeare was born in 1564, Tree had grown quite tall and thick; she matured and began to drop cones in the appropriate season.

Tree had not experienced earlier times, but older trees, taught by yet older trees, said that pines had stood in this area for thousands of years: living, dying, falling, rotting back into the soil. Those generations of trees had seen Native People come and go during the summer, digging pits to obtain the red metal—copper—found close to the surface, perhaps as early as 2000 years BCE. The older trees passing on this knowledge did not know why those people stopped coming to the area, but they left the trees, plants and numerous animals undisturbed for centuries. Then, other humans of the Ojibwa tribe began to visit, paddling along the shore of Gitchi Gumee in their birch bark canoes.

Tree, and those around her, watched generation after generation of deer, bear, wolves, chipmunks, squirrels, countless birds and other animals raise their families, gather nuts, eat the vegetation and prey upon each other in their efforts to survive. These dramatic acts repeated themselves season after season, century after century.

Tree lived on, not knowing until her growth rings marked the year later for people to count them; that St. Peter's Basilica was built as she grew taller and her trunk thickened between 1600 and 1626; that early colonists from England began to settle the Atlantic Coast far from the Keweenaw, or how they struggled to survive; that Sir Isaac Newton, an important scientist of his age, credited with "discovering" how gravity worked, was born in 1643. Tree did note, though, that when the oldest trees died, they always fell downhill. She didn't know at the time that another ring marked the year 1685, when Johann Sebastian Bach was born, or that Mozart wrote his first opera, around 1770, at the tender age of fourteen. Tree did know the music of the birds, the rhythm of waves crashing on the Lake Superior shore and the whistle of the wind through her branches at various speeds.

Tree had watched as other people with lighter skin came in large canoes to trade with the Ojibwa. She watched the populations of furbearing animals dwindle as they were hunted along streams running through the forest, and trees in the forests throughout the region reported similar stories. She also saw that these light-skinned people left the Ojibwa sick and dying with diseases they spread unintentionally. Trees that grew closer to the shores where trading took place noted that the light-skinned people tended to end up with the larger share in any trade.

How else might these new people change my world? she wondered. Somewhere around 1762, lightning struck, and a terrible fire raged over the end of the Keweenaw Peninsula, destroying acres and acres of forest, but Tree survived. She watched with great joy over the next few decades as seedlings began to sprout, not just pines, but also cedar, yellow birch, red oak, sugar maple and balsam fir. Some eighty-five species of birds, twenty-three species of ferns and orchids and many other plants became part of her forest. Tree passed along her history and the collected knowledge of the forest to these young trees.

July 4, 1776, was just another summer day for Tree when men gathered in Philadelphia, Pennsylvania, to declare themselves a new nation, independent from England. Tree knew some of the war and struggle that followed, because by this time, her roots had spread out enough to hear of events from distant places through the network of intermingled roots, not unlike the imagined trees of Pandora in the movie *Avatar*. She had communicated with other trees close to her for almost three centuries already and now, her world grew.

Tree was not concerned with the fact that the United States purchased half a continent in 1803, or that Napoleon was defeated at Waterloo in 1815. Perhaps she should have been; these new people were ambitious beyond imagining, which can be good, or bad, depending upon whether or not you are a tree in their way. These new people certainly had less respect for the land and living creatures than the Ojibwa did.

Many more people began to arrive in larger boats and ships not far away at a place these people called Copper Harbor. They began a "copper rush" several years before the California Gold Rush. These people began digging copper from deep underground, all along the spine of the Keweenaw, well ahead of those more famous people who raced to the west coast of the continent. The new people used better technology than those early copper diggers who dug only crude pits. Tree and the other pines watched as many of their not-too-distant cousins were cut down for timber. The peninsula would never be the same again.

Over the next decades, copper from those mines was shipped down the Great Lakes while Darwin wrote *The Origin of the Species* in 1859. The root network reported that copper mixed with other metals provided weapons for the Union during the American Civil War. Tree watched as more and more of the forest disappeared, but there were still many trees easier to reach than those in the grove where she grew. The rugged land at the tip of the Keweenaw kept people away during those years.

A few people did enter Tree's part of the forest to dig for copper. They named themselves the Diamond Drilling Camp, but they had only a single cabin and a stable. Tree and those near her watched with a greater level of concern than they had before. But these people didn't last long. While folks in Copper Harbor managed to make it through the brutal winters experienced on the Keweenaw, those of the Diamond Drilling Camp gave up when they found there was not enough copper in this forest to make it worth the effort.

Tree didn't care that the intercontinental railroad was completed in 1869, but the more immediate root system let her know that the iron rails reached places not too far from her and that there were important changes not far away. Forests in other areas fell to the axe to build people's homes and shore up the tunnels they dug in the earth more quickly than the trees could grow back. She did hear through the root line that Yellowstone Park was established in 1872, showing that at least some people were beginning to see the need to preserve a bit of the continent's plants and animals.

But the year before, Tree had heard that forests not very far from her had been mowed down to nothing, sending shivers through the branches of the forest. She also noticed that other men with huge saws looked at the pines near where she grew and saw only board feet of lumber, not the ecosystem the forest provided. Later, news came back that one of the reasons so many beautiful pines had gone down was that a great city people referred to as "Chicago" had burned nearly to the ground. That caused a huge demand for timber to rebuild—timber that came from the forests of Michigan's Upper Peninsula. Tree learned that her species was especially prized for construction because their trunks grew tall, thick and straight.

The pines around Tree didn't make much note that children's author E.B. White was born in 1899, or that White would gain much acclaim for a book, *Charlotte's Web*, that would make one six-year-old girl begin to think about the importance and lives of creatures besides her and would later tell Tree's story. Tree didn't have much interest in the fact that the Wright Brothers flew into the sky at Kitty Hawk in 1903, or that another famous American author, Mark Twain, died in 1910, but she noted that many men left the area to fight in what the forest heard was called the Great War a few years later.

Tree had a huge diameter by 1942 when she heard, through the forest network, that many more men left the area to fight in what the people called World War II. The forest network relayed how important the copper and iron resources of Michigan's Upper Peninsula were to the people of the many nations fighting that war. It was but a distant concept to Tree and those around her. She did notice, however, that she hadn't seen any wolves run along the forest floor chasing deer or moose in quite a while.

But in 1970, a power saw ground into Tree's huge trunk and down she went. She groaned and her crash echoed over the hills and gullies, enough to anger many people who took action. Somehow, a group of them managed to obtain a slice from Tree's trunk. When they counted back her growth rings, they were amazed, and Tree finally learned all the human history that had taken place during her years of life. This group of people worked together to stop the saws in that part of the forest. The group had a name: the Michigan Nature Association. They bought the land with its trees—200 acres—and then more over subsequent years, totaling over 500 acres. They preserved the land and the trees so the animals, birds and plants could thrive there forever and named the sanctuary after the land's previous owner, Edward Adolph Joseph Estivant.

With great care, these people built trails through the sanctuary so that all could enjoy and appreciate the forest. The crosscut from Tree became a display at the trail head with her growth rings labeled, so all who saw it could begin to realize the specialness of this precious old growth forest at the tip of Michigan's Keweenaw. You can visit Tree, her brothers, sisters, cousins and descendants at Estivant Pines, near Copper Harbor, by following US41 and turning right on Second St., following the signs to Lake Manganese and a waterfall and then continuing along a dirt road with signs saying "E Pines" pointing the way to the trail head.

Experience, learn, appreciate, imagine.

To join or support the Michigan Nature Association, 2310 Science Parkway, Suite 100, Okemos, Michigan 48864 or call 866-223-2231. See www.SuperiorTapestry.com/sites for more info including a short video overview.

Chapter 22 – Fireside Stories of Hearth and Home

Fig. 22-1: Officers' Quarters at Fort Wilkins State Historical Park

Fireplace as she stands today in the kitchen of one of the officers' quarters at Fort Wilkins State Historical Park.

The bricks for Hearth had made a long and difficult journey from their place of origin to the wilderness at Copper Harbor. There, they were mortared together into a kitchen fireplace in what was becoming one of the officer's quarters at Fort- Wilkins. As her chimney rose, Hearth watched the two companies of the U.S. Army that arrived there in May of 1844. Officers talked about their mission to keep the peace between an influx of white people trying to establish copper mining in the area and the Ojibwa people who already lived there. But Hearth never saw any problems between those two groups.

Hearth watched their field exercises and saw some leave for guard duty, but wondered what they were guarding the others from. The main task of the soldiers that summer was building cabins and other needed structures to live in before the first snow of winter. Soldiers came back from their walks to the town of Copper Harbor, which consisted of a few buildings and warehouses, scattered log houses, a general store and a building for the United States Mineral Land Agency Office. She learned that all local buildings were built of logs cut from the surrounding forests and chunks of native rock. Hearth could not see the village or Lake Superior from where she was, but she had a wonderful view of an inland lake right in front of the fort. Vivid hues of red, orange, yellow and gold highlighted the deep green of spruce and pine when fall came. The men raved about it, too, and Hearth now recognized different accents among the soldiers and local residents: mostly Irish, German or Cornish at that time.

One day, the camp commander said to one of the other officers, "This tiny village is a point of rendezvous and supply for the rough mining camps along the cliffs. We are more of a police force to their challenges of the rules of civilization than we are a protecting force."

Hearth, as part of the fireplace around her, knew she had an important job as the center of the home for heat and cooking. She was glad to be built of good-quality brick. While cook stoves were certainly available in many areas of the country, they were hard to ship to the Copper Harbor wilderness. Fireplace cooking was still the norm in all military installations. Hearth watched as other similar fireplaces went up for the other officer's quarters, married enlisted men's cottages and the camp kitchens.

A swinging handle with a large hook on it was embedded into her bricks so the women of the house could hang pots and kettles of various sizes over the fire, and then be swung out to stir whatever was in the pot or serve it onto plates or into bowls. Hearth was a little fancier than fireplaces in the married enlisted men's quarters. She had painted wood panels along the outer edges and a similarly painted mantle above. Those in the married enlisted men's quarters had only bricks for the mantle.

Once Hearth was complete, she watched the rest of the building go up around her. Two officers' families had quarters within the building, each with a parlor, dining room, kitchen (where Hearth stood) and sleeping rooms upstairs. But for most of the year, people spent the bulk of their time in the warmest place, the kitchen. She reveled in being the center of attention and in the "Huums" and "Ahhs" over the hearty soups and stews bubbling in kettles hanging over her fire.

Hearth admired the women who had to manage everything. Cooking over an open fire could be a tricky process. She was delighted to hear that her mistress, Richardetta Hooe—whose lilting tongue revealed that she hailed from Virginia—had married First Lieutenant Daniel Ruggles in 1841. She already knew when more wood needed to be added to boil meat before adding vegetables to the stew, when the coals were just right to bury a Dutch oven in them to bake biscuits or a pie, or when to place a drip pan under roasting meat, hissing as it turned on a spit. Hearth's mistress saved those drippings for special flavor in any food and to fry other foods later.

One day, Richardetta reprimanded a soldier who brought her a load of wood. "Not just any wood will do for a cooking fire. I need hardwoods like oak, hickory, maple, ash or dogwood. There are plenty of such trees here. Blazing flames might look pretty, but they are not as good for cooking and heating as red-hot coals."

"Sorry Ma'am. I'll get what you want."

Richardetta lit that kitchen fire early every morning in order to have cooking coals by breakfast time. There was not a lot of variation in the meals prepared over Hearth—mostly soups, stews, berry pies in the summer, apples in the fall, pottages, oatmeal, beans and the like—but they were hearty and nutritious. Hearth heard her mistress say more than once that she was glad that, with their higher officers' pay, she could afford to buy more items at the Sutler's Store than enlisted men. That meant they had more meat than other families. Hearth didn't have to bake bread, since all the bread for the entire fort came from the ovens in the fort bakery. Often, they had a treat of deer meat, wild turkey, rabbit or other game shot by officers and men.

Besides the lieutenant and his wife, Mrs. Ruggles' teenaged sister, Fanny Hooe, stayed with them, and there were two hired servants.

John Singer and Julia Sutherland helped around the place and kept Mrs. Ruggles' one-year-old son from crawling too close to Hearth. At the evening meal, Hearth could hear Lieutenant Ruggles tell stories about his eleven years in the army—especially the years he had served on the Wisconsin frontier or during the Seminole Indian War in Florida. Hearth stared in fascination on winter nights when Daniel Ruggles spread out one of his scientific projects. Interested in geology, he collected several important rock samples, which he sent to the National Institute. He finally had time to explain to his wife his summer and fall studies of the rising and falling of Lake Superior to see if he could observe any tidal influences. "No evidence of tides," he said.

First Lieutenant Carter Stevenson often joined Ruggles to discuss what was going on at the fort, and Stevenson's wife, Martha, spent many hours with Richardetta. Back while the fort was still under construction, the two officers, under the direction of their captain, had set up a daily schedule for the men, combining regular army routines with those of building the structures they needed to live in: Reveille at sunrise; fatigue for twenty minutes; breakfast at 7am, fatigue again at 7:30am; orderly at noon, assembly at 12:30pm; dinner at 1pm, fatigue again at 1:30pm; assembly again pre-sunset; retreat at sunset; tattoo at 9pm. As the summer wore into fall, sunrise came later and sunset earlier. A household schedule for Hearth was similar, except that her work started well ahead of any meal.

The two officers discussed many things in front of Hearth. Would the last supply boats arrive in time? Well, they could certainly supplement their meat supply by hunting. That would keep some of the men busy, too. How many pairs of boots were in the Sutler's Store? Were there enough beer and tobacco? How many jars of pickles? Barrels of flour? Enough hay for the sheep and cattle they would slaughter and eat during the winter? Nothing would come into Copper Harbor once the snows began and ice covered the harbor. Every Sunday afternoon, the two officers would decide who went to inspect the enlisted men's quarters and the squad room. Yes, their fort was more casual than most army forts, but they did need a certain level of discipline. Habitual drunkenness and "general worthlessness" overcame many of the men as the winter wore on— more than one man ended up in the guard house.

One evening, Stevenson laughed and said, "Would you believe, I heard one of the men complain that he had joined the army in order to avoid getting a job? 'Now I have to do three or four times as much work as I joined the army to get out of,' I heard him grumble. What was he thinking?"

When Captain Robert Clary joined them, he often reminded his officers, "Tell the men that their quarters—and yours, too—are as good and comfortable as any in the army." Hearth knew that the three officers got on together well because they had much in common. All three had graduated from West Point Military Academy.

"This winter boredom, stuck inside so much, is hard on the men, I have to admit," Captain Clary said.

The two lieutenants nodded.

Winter did bring some surprises and blessings, though. Richardetta gave birth to another baby boy in December. All the wives in the fort came to congratulate her and help out. Hearth was very busy, as other women cooked over her. Then in January, Father Baraga arrived at the fort. Everyone was amazed that he had made such a long, difficult and tedious journey on snowshoes to be there and minister to them.

"It's seventy or eighty miles from L'Anse through the woods in deep snow!" Stevenson said. "How does he do it?"

Hearth was honored that the priest stayed with her lieutenant and his wife for several days. Besides holding services, Father Baraga baptized four babies, listened to confessions, gave out Holy Communion and everything else he could to minister to both Catholics and Protestants. Everyone spoke of him with great respect. Hearth wasn't present at the baptisms, which took place in the parlors and the smaller cottages of the married enlisted men, but she could hear his gracious words in the dining room during the evening meal. Hearth also heard that Lieutenant Ruggles stood as godfather to one of the enlisted men's babies. The winter seemed less drab when Father Baraga was with them.

As the winter wore on, Hearth witnessed the fact that the ladies of her home dumped more and more garbage into one corner of the cellar beneath the kitchen—it was simply too cold to carry it to the fort dump. In the spring, no one even went down the ladder to get to the cellar, because several inches of water from snow-melt had seeped in, making it unusable for quite a while.

At long last, Hearth could hear birds twittering. A veil of green lace draped the trees and, with it, more joy at the arrival of the Stevensons' baby. But two months later, grief came when the baby died. Richardetta spent a great deal of time with her friend, Martha, comforting her. Hearth wanted to cry, too.

The top of Hearth's chimney watched the soldiers plant a vegetable garden in the spring. However, the soil there was thin, rocky and barren. The potatoes and other root vegetables planted there did not grow well. Hearth continued to see the last of the previous fall's potato supply (most with spots of gray) peeled, trimmed of the rotten spots and dumped into a pot on the hook.

Seemingly as quickly as Ft. Wilkins had been built, its garrison was transferred south to aid in the Mexican-American war. Hearth wept as Richardetta and the other wives packed up their personal belongings to have them shipped to yet another post, but the women seemed to accept sudden transfers like this. A new company arrived, but their numbers were fewer and the stories not as interesting, at least in Hearth's opinion. Then in 1847, the fort was closed completely. A dejected Hearth sat collecting dust and cobwebs for several years.

From 1855 to 1861, Doctor Livermore rented the fort for a summer health spa. People came during the warmer months to rest refresh themselves in the fresh clean air and sunshine. Hearth enjoyed these summer people and dreaded when they left each fall, because all winter, she remained cold and unused. The good doctor died in 1861 and Hearth was lonelier than ever.

When the Civil War ended, the United States Army found it had too many men whose enlistments were not yet up, and those men needed to be sent somewhere. Fort Wilkins was opened again with many enlisted men, some married, and a new group of officers, wives and families. Work detail, drill, work detail, drill, inspection, work detail, drill, keep the men busy, don't let them drink too much...all over again. Captain Kenelm Robbins ran as tight a post as was possible in non-war circumstances. Hearth was thrilled to have a woman to tend a cooking fire again. She was even more thrilled when the captain's wife, Alice, gave birth to their daughter, Matilda.

Alice's friends in Copper Harbor included such copper pioneers and residents as Daniel and Lucena Brockway and Henry Selby, the local mine agent. Hearth helped put on many parties and turkey dinners. She listened as the couples enjoyed card games in the parlor. Laughter, and sometimes singing, floated into the kitchen.

Shipping was better and faster since the opening of the first state lock at Sault Ste. Marie. However, there was still one very difficult winter, when the last boat to go through that lock filled with winter supplies for Copper Harbor and Fort Wilkins foundered in one of those infamous November gales. Hearth watched as the stews cooked over her coals had more water and less and less meat and vegetables. The women cut the camp bakery's loaves into ever thinner slices. Before the first boat of late spring finally came, she noticed that officers and men who came into the kitchen had longer ends hanging from their belt buckles and the ties at the back of the women's aprons draped low. Hollowed cheeks in their faces became more noticeable.

Hearth listened to one interesting scandal. Officers learned that James Flynn, who had just been named a first sergeant, was not who he said he was and had a "checkered past." He was really John Power. He had enlisted in the army at the age of seventeen to fight in the Civil War, served honorably and was discharged. Then, he re-enlisted but deserted his unit only three months later. At Fort Wilkins, he finally admitted his deceit. He and Captain Robbins worked out a way for him to finish his enlistment without a court martial. He finished his service honorably, was discharged and chose to remain in Copper Harbor as a civilian.

It didn't take many years, though, for all those Civil War veterans to end their enlistments and head home. In 1870, Fort Wilkins received word that it would be closed permanently.

Hearth cried.

For a while each summer, the site was used as a casual camping place, but nobody used Hearth. Most of the buildings were closed and locked up tight. Again, winters were especially lonely. A man named Judson P. North renovated several of the buildings in 1900-1901, hoping to establish a summer resort, but his plans failed. For the next two decades, Hearth looked at bare walls and occasionally heard sounds in the summer when a few people came to picnic, or between 1913 and 1919, when a man from Calumet rented two of the buildings for a hunting camp. *Dull*, thought Hearth. *When will someone cook over me again?*

The federal government planned to "dispose of" the site, but Hearth was saved when a group from Houghton and Keweenaw Counties bought the land in 1921. Just two years later, they turned it over to the State of Michigan as a state park. Different groups of people worked on restoration over the years until Fort Wilkins became what it is today—a summer place of living history and learning.

Even though no one actually cooks over Hearth any more, she is content to have summer visitors see what she looked like from the 1840s to the 1860s. She has learned that she can last through the lonely winters by hibernating like so many animals. She's glad to see people return at the end of May every year to look through the glass to see what a kitchen looked like long ago.

Visit Hearth at Fort Wilkins Historic State Park, 15223 US 41, Copper Harbor, Michigan, 49918. For more information including a brief video tour, visit www.SuperiorTapestry.com/sites.

.

Chapter 23 – Famous Float Copper

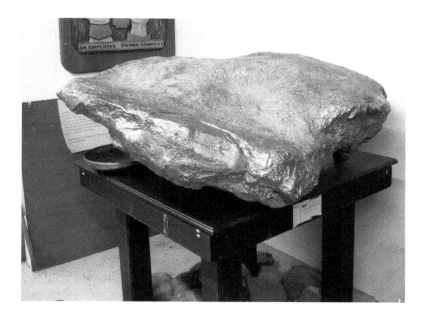

Fig. 23-1: Replica of the Ontonagon Boulder

This is a replica of the Ontonagon Boulder. To see the "real thing," you must travel to the Smithsonian Institution, though it is not always on display.

Ontonagon Boulder formed over millions of years in the same process that formed the Basalt Sisters. Heat from the magma forced water between and through these formations. Water leached and changed these rocks and spaces. Hot fluid then filled the spaces, holes, and pipes, leaving mineral deposits behind: copper and small amounts of gold and silver, along with other trace minerals.

Especially copper.

Ontonagon Boulder was one of those patient deposits of pure native copper waiting far below the earth's surface to see daylight, one way or another. It was only during the fourth glacial age that Ontonagon Boulder reached the top, to be greeted by tons of ice gouging along the surface of the earth. The force of the ice broke Boulder away from the rest of the copper vein and dragged her, quite against her will. The pressure and dragging were so painful! Gradually, the pressure lessened. A blue glow appeared above her, growing brighter over many years. The glacier melted away, leaving her behind on the shore of a river of melt water. There she sat, enjoying the sun in summer, watching grass, and then trees, grow along the riverbank. Living things wandered by. Wolves, bears, deer, moose and many smaller animals sniffed at her and walked away. Birds perched upon her to rest.

Boulder enjoyed the arrival and passing of each season. Wicked winds whipped around, emptying the trees of leaves in fall, to be followed by gentle or blizzard snows, then the melting and greening of the land followed by warm sun and rain, rainbows of flowers, cooling breezes, bright blasts of fall color and a repeat of autumn winds.

Native Peoples believed that pieces of copper left on the surface, from small nuggets to huge chunks like Boulder weighing thousands of pounds, housed kind spirits. Pieces that were small enough to be easily carried were treasured, wrapped in furs, and later cloth, and passed down from generation to generation. The Native Peoples worshipped larger pieces, like Boulder, that could not be moved from their resting places along river banks, in forests or meadows.

The Ojibwa clans came to lift up their hearts to Boulder; they honored her, touched her reverently. This made her feel special, somehow more valuable than the river, or the smaller rocks around her, or even the trees. The Ojibwa never tried to break off parts of her, or damage her in any way. People had dug other pieces of copper from pits, formed the red metal into bowls, ornaments and jewelry, but not a bit did they ever take from Boulder.

Time marched on. Boulder began to see a different kind of human visit her. These people did not venerate the massive chunk of copper. They wanted to own her, or at least a piece of her. She heard them call her by various names: the Copper Rock of Lake Superior, then later the Ontonagon Boulder.

Boulder liked having a name, but she didn't like what these new people did. In 1766, Alexander Henry, a Mackinac trader, traveled many miles from the Straights of Mackinaw and portaged up the St. Mary's River into Lake Superior. Then he paddled hundreds of miles more to the mouth of the Ontonagon River and finally thirty miles up the river to reach the place. Boulder was flattered by the story this man and those with him told, but could see a look in their eyes that frightened her, a look far different from the worship of the Ojibwa. He hacked at Boulder until he managed to cut off a 100-pound piece from her and carried it away, leaving a dull ache and a lasting scar.

Alexander Henry was not the only man to break off a chunk. When two other famous men, Douglass Houghton and Henry Rowe Schoolcraft, visited Boulder, they reported many axe and chisel marks all over her. Covered with these scars, Boulder was ashamed of her looks. She wondered if these people cut off parts of each other, but they all seemed whole. Much to Boulder's relief, Houghton did not harm her. But later, she learned that his purpose was to map out the geology of Michigan's Upper Peninsula, so that people could begin to develop the areas where copper and iron resided in the ground.

Then men tried to do more than cut off chunks. They attempted to move her! When no amount of prying budged her, stubborn female that she was, they piled some thirty cords of wood around her and set them ablaze. Then, they threw water on the heated copper, hoping to fracture it. Boulder had felt much worse heat and cold than that over eons of her existence. Not a thing resulted from that attempt. She gave these men a disgusting but also pitiful look, which, of course, they could not see. A second expedition a couple of years later also failed miserably, but did manage to move Boulder four or five feet.

Yet another man came in 1841. Julius Eldred, a hardware merchant from Detroit, wanted to own the Ontonagon Boulder, remove her from the area and have people pay to see her. Julius had a trading license from the United States Government, and as such, he "bought" Boulder from the Ojibwa for $150.00 ($45.00 of it in cash and the rest in goods to be delivered in two years). Unfortunately for Julius (but momentary good fortune for Boulder), he learned that the land on which Boulder sat belonged to someone else! So, in 1843, Julius was forced to pay an additional $1365.00 in order to retain possession of Boulder.

Now Eldred faced the problem of moving the over-3000-pound mass!

"Ha," Boulder thought. "What makes you think you can move me after all the others failed?"

Boulder watched somewhat curiously as a crew of twenty-one men built a sectional, portable railway and flat car. They used capstans, block and tackle dragged over a four-and-a-half-mile right-of-way over hills and through dense forest to a navigable part of the Ontonagon River. Boulder heard a man named General Walter Cunningham, US Mineral agent for the region, say that it was "one of the most extraordinary performances of the age."

Boulder did her best to be as stubborn as she had been with all other attempts. It took Eldred two tries with all that equipment, but he got her onto the skid, from there to the flat rail car and on down the river to the shore of Lake Superior and onto a ship. The cheering and excitement of the men at this accomplishment amazed Boulder enough that she decided she might as well enjoy the ride and see what other adventures were in store for her.

Eldred was quite rightly proud of himself, picturing all the money he could make charging twenty-five cents per person to see this wonderful solid mass of copper! Then, General Cunningham informed Eldred, and Boulder learned as she listened during the ship's voyage back to Detroit, that his whole purpose for watching the incredible movement of Boulder was because he had been ordered by Secretary of War, James M. Porter, to seize Boulder for the United States Government.

The sharp words that followed left Boulder wondering what was to become of her. Words like "stealing," "against the law," "bought and paid for," "see you in court" (and other phrases not meant for polite conversation) flew between the two men.

Porter had stated:

> "The Persons claiming the rock have no right to it, but justice and equity would require that they be amply compensated for the trouble and expense of its removal from its position on the Ontonagon to the lake; and for this purpose, General Cunningham will examine their accounts

and allow them the costs, compensating them fully and fairly, the sum, however, not to exceed $700.00."

Eldred shouted the math. He was out $150, plus another $1345.00, plus all the pay for the men and cost of the equipment... Boulder heard him yelling the most impolite words about going to court! The Secretary of War finally did give Eldred a total of $5,664.98.

Eldred was only able to display Boulder from Oct. 11, 1843 until Nov. 1, 1843. Boulder actually enjoyed being on display. These people weren't worshiping her as the Ojibwa had, but they certainly "oooed" and "ahhhed" enough to give her a sense of pride. They didn't seem to notice her scars. Most importantly, no one was trying to break off any more pieces!

On November the 9th, Boulder began her journey from Detroit to Washington, D.C. She expected another grand display, but she ended up sitting in the yard of the Quartermaster's Bureau of the War Department until 1855. Then, they moved her to storage in the Patent Office!

What disappointment and insult!

Finally, in 1858, Boulder was sent to the U.S. National Museum, where she was admired again. Her residence since November of 1971 had been in the Smithsonian Institution. At that time, the copper in her was estimated to be worth $1,590.00. Boulder laughs at the irony every time she is moved from storage to display and back to storage.

Boulder has heard, however, that a larger Float Copper cousin weighing over 9000 pounds was found buried under four and a half feet of glacial till, the soil dragged along beneath a glacier, about four miles southwest of Calumet, Michigan. This cousin is proudly displayed at the corner of US 41 and Red Jacket Road on a lovely green near what once was the Calumet Public Library and now houses the archives of the Keweenaw National Historical Park, and across Red Jacket Road from the Keweenaw National Historical Park headquarters building. Visitors can see this cousin for free, not far from where that mass of float copper lay in the ground a bit longer than the Ontonagon Boulder.

People may also visit a replica of the Ontonagon Boulder at the Ontonagon County Historical Society Museum, 422 River St. Ontonagon Michigan, Ph. 906-884-6165, hours: Nov. – Apr.

Thursday-Sat. 10-4; May- Oct. Tues.- Sat. 10-4. For more info
please visit www.SuperiorTapestry.com/sites.

Fig. 23-2: Another example of float copper

Ontonagon Boulder's cousin at the corner of US 41 and Red Jacket Road in
Calumet, Michigan.

Chapter 24 – Toppling Timber

The old sawyer carried dull, two-man Saw into the blacksmith's shop. "Any hope to recut these teeth again before this season's cutting starts?" he asked the smith. He had taken Saw there many times over the years.

The smith took six-foot Saw, still slightly wider in the middle than at its tapered ends, wooden handles at each end, from his old friend. "Hate to say this, but there's not enough width at the ends for another cutting of new teeth."

A sigh from the old sawyer. "I was afraid that might be, but just hoping I could get one more season out of it."

"I know what you mean. Got some new sheets of spring steel here, though—could make you a new one, use your old handles. I can use the iron in the old saw to make other things. Give you some credit for that."

Another sigh from the old sawyer, then he lifted his hands in resignation. "Guess that's the best move. My grandson, Jack, is coming out with me this year, since I'm teaching him the trade. He'll start his years off with a new saw, I guess."

"Great start for him, *ja*. Good thing you got that grandson since all you had was girls. Stop back next week this time and I'll have it ready for you."

The old sawyer nodded and left.

During the next few days, the blacksmith cut a wide strip from one sheet of spring steel. He carefully shaped and cut the teeth into it, set the angle of each, and checked the depth of the rakers, shorter teeth that scraped the sawdust out of a tree rather than cutting into it. He removed the handles from the old saw and attached into them firmly to the new one, talking to himself as he did so.

Fig. 24-1: Cross-cut saw at Ontonagon County Historical Museum

An undignified end to a cross-cut saw, pinched in a tree by the users' foolishness

As the smith talked to himself, Saw learned that they were several years into the Twentieth Century. Lumbering had been going on in the Ontonagon area for many years already—the demand for the straight, strong beams from the area's white pines having jumped by leaps and bounds after the great fire of Chicago. Saw heard the smith continue to muse about how much longer things could go on, though. Small lumber companies, run by men like Georgy Sission and Francis Lilly, had done a fine job with the area's forests for many years. Then, the big Diamond Match Company had taken out options on so many parcels of land that they were able to control the business and shut out smaller producers. That company's push for greater production and poor management of slashed branches left behind had resulted in a great fire that had destroyed the Diamond Match Company's sawmills and most of the Village of Ontonagon in 1896. The old saw could have told the new one about that difficult time for the people of the area, but that old saw had already been repurposed into other useful items, so the smith's musings did the job instead.

The smith felt grateful that his building had been spared from the fire. The rest of the town was still recovering from the loss. The smith, nearly as old as his sawyer friend, remembered the days when all people could see along the Ontonagon River were forests: great stands of white pine, maple, oak, ash, hemlock, poplar and aspen. Now, the forests that were left grew farther and farther from the town and the river. Trees went down much faster than they grew. The wonderful stands of white pine had all but disappeared and the last of the great river drives had taken place in 1895. Lesser amounts of the maple and oak were shipped out by rail to make into furniture. "How much longer?" the smith said out loud.

Late in the week toward evening, the smith talked to the metal he worked and tempered. "Got to get your teeth just right. Want you to cut a lot of trees for my friend and be a good tool for his grandson as long as possible. Don't want you messing up and breaking. You got to keep up my good name." Saw nodded in his own way.

The week passed and Saw was ready. When the sawyer arrived, he had his grandson with him. "So, this is the young man about to enter a lumber camp. Good to meet you, Jack." The smith reached out his rough hand to shake that of a boy he judged to be about sixteen, but now a man in the eyes of the community.

"Yup, he'll be working this new saw with me this winter, then finding himself a new partner next. Now, we just wait for the cold and snow so we can get to work."

The old sawyer showed Jack how to carry the saw balanced over his shoulder, and then he and his grandfather left the blacksmith shop. Saw looked around as they walked along. In addition to a couple of saloons, store fronts lined the sides of the main street. Tidy houses lined up behind them on one side, with the river running behind the stores on the west side. Wind whistled down the street and Saw could hear waves crashing behind them on the Lake Superior shore. They walked a mile or so out of town and hung Saw carefully in the family barn before going into their homes. The old man lived with his wife in a log cabin on one side of the barn. His oldest daughter and her husband had a snug frame house on the other side of the barn and farmed the open land around the two simple homes. The other daughter and her husband lived in town, where they ran a general store.

Finally, the day came when the old sawyer and the boy headed off to the lumber camp. They would stay there all winter, cutting trees, sleeping in the bunk house and eating whatever the camp cook put on the long plank tables.

Along the way, the old sawyer explained to his grandson what he could expect to see. "There's lots of different men at the camp. There's the 'monkeys' who pick up horse droppings; those who pour water on the trails to ice them down so the logs we cut slide easily; there's the horses with their drivers pulling the huge bobsleds loaded with the logs we cut. None of them can work without us sawyers. But mind you, always do exactly what the boss says—that is if you want to keep working. Some bosses is nice; others, not so much. We got a good one in this camp, so let him know you'll work hard and appreciate him. Oh, and never complain about the food, unless you want to go hungry. Most of the time, you'll be so hungry you won't care anyways."

The old man showed Jack around the camp and introduced him. After a hearty supper, they entered the bunk house, which was not much warmer than it was outside in the snow, in spite of a potbellied stove at one end. Both the old man and the young one climbed onto their plank bunks—the young man on the top—and rolled themselves up fully clothed in the blankets they had brought.

The next day began very early. Having filled their bellies with flapjacks smothered in maple syrup, salt pork, biscuits and coffee, the pair headed out into the woods, carrying Saw. He could not help but feel excited at the idea of being used for his intended purpose.

When they reached a fine, tall white pine with a decent-sized trunk, the old man stopped. He pulled a pint bottle of coal oil from a large front pocket in his jacket and demonstrated how to lubricate the blade. "Never forget this step," he instructed. "Got to keep the blade oiled. Don't want it to get stuck half way through the tree." He pulled the cork with his teeth and poured a bit of it along the blade, then rubbed it along the saw's teeth with a rag he took from his other front pocket. Finally, he popped the cork back in (it had remained between his teeth all this time) and returned the oil flask to his pocket.

Then, he took the small axe he carried on his belt and cut a notch in one side of the tree. "That notch is so the tree will fall that way." He pointed in the direction that he wanted the tree to fall.

"Take that end," he instructed. "You never *push* the saw, you only *pull* it, and I only pull it. Side to side, nice and easy but quickly—we want to cut as many trees as possible each day. We probably will spend most of today with you getting in rhythm with me. But tomorrow, we got to move quicker."

Jack nodded.

"Put these wedges in your pocket. I'll tell you when to use them. When I say to stop, stop!"

The old man started slowly, patient with his grandson, set the saw to the trunk of the tree and the rhythm began slowly. The saw's teeth ripped through the outer bark, great chips falling into the snow. Jack tried to push the saw only once. The rebuke from his grandfather reminded him *never* to do that again if he wanted to continue as an apprentice sawyer.

Sawdust fell from the growing kerf, the cut into the tree, into the snow with each pull on Saw. *This is what I was made for*, Saw thought. He loved the sound he made as the two men pulled in turn. Grimmm, Grimmm... almost like humming. With each pull, his teeth cut deeper and deeper into the tree. Just when Saw would have disappeared into the wood, the old man signaled to stop. "We got to put a wedge in here," he said. "It will hold the kerf open and begin to make the tree tilt the way we notched."

Wedge tapped in place with the side of the ax, the two pulled Saw back and forth again, the rhythm increasing slightly as the young man began to feel it. Soon, it was time for another wedge, then another and about three quarters of the way through the thick trunk, another.

Back and forth, back and forth. The sawdust continued to pile up. Saw could feel the tree beginning to give way, even before the first cracking sound—the tree seemed to shudder as he ground his way through the trunk.

Then the C-R-A-C-K!

"TIMBER!" shouted the old man. The tree fell exactly where he wanted it.

Other men took over and began trimming the branches with axes, preparing it to be pulled behind the bobsled to a location where each log would be marked with the company and sawyer's signs. They threw all the slash into piles on the snow-covered ground.

"Come on," said the old man. "On to the next one, but faster this time. You learning good."

Occasionally, but only occasionally, the pair took a break to drink a slug of coffee from a thermos and later to gobble up some sandwiches that had been prepared by the cook and handed out that morning and which they had carried in their pockets.

"Sure am glad some smart guy invented this here thermos a few years ago! Sure comes in handy to get a hot drink," Grandfather said.

Saw appreciated these breaks, since heat built up along his teeth in spite of the cold temperatures. Throughout the day, the pair spattered more oil onto Saw. He could sense when Jack began to tire. The boy's breathing increased; he huffed and puffed as he pulled on the handle. The old man, however, never seemed to tire.

At the end of the day, the old man introduced young Jack to the camp "dentist," a specialist in each logging camp who sharpened the saw teeth at the end of each day. This same man also rotated the handles of one saw with another pair so the handles wore evenly by being in the hands of different sawyers from time to time.

Tree after tree, day after day. Only during the worst blizzards did the lumbermen stay inside the bunk house or chow hall. All the men in the camp would be paid at the end of the season according to how much work the camp accomplished, how many logs lay in piles, waiting for spring temperatures to thaw the ice on the river. That cash the men earned had to last all summer and fall, until it was time to cut trees again.

About half way through the winter, Saw began to notice that Jack no longer huffed and puffed as the day wore on. Now, it was the old man who began to slow down the rhythm of pull, pause, pull, pause. Saw also noticed that the pair talked less and less. The old man simply knew when to stop to oil the saw's teeth; Jack seemed to feel when his grandfather needed to rest. They were a perfect team.

When the winter finally ended, the old man collected his pay. He counted out one third of it and handed it to his grandson. "Don't spend this in the saloons like you see some of these men do on the way home," he stated. "You give it to your parents and then they'll let you keep some for yourself. Next winter, one of them branch cutters will probably be your partner. You'll work it out with him how much he gets. But you get more because you are already a good sawyer. Teach him good, and you'll have a partner for life at work."

"I will, Gramps," Jack said, as he lifted Saw to his shoulder. The air was warmer. Trees dripped with melting snow and patches of bare ground showed here and there.

"Look, Gramps, a robin!"

"Yup. Spring is here."

The two hiked the miles back to the homes they'd left in the late fall. As they walked along the river toward town, the logs they had cut floated gently in the current, to be gathered at the harbor and shipped out. But the river was not nearly as thick with logs as it had once been. Some would go by boat to other ports on Lake Superior. Some logs would be loaded onto rail cars to other places, where they would be cut into timber for construction.

Jack hung Saw in the barn. There he stayed while the weather grew warmer and warmer. Saw began to understand that the young girl who came in every morning and night to milk the cow was Jack's younger sister. The snow gave way to green grass. The family cow went out into the meadow, but the girl brought the cow in every morning and evening. Saw did not know what the buckets of milk were for.

Late in the summer, Saw observed through the open barn door that the family carried an oblong box from the log cabin to a place under a large oak tree where the cow liked to lie in the heat of midday. They dug a deep hole and lowered the box into it. Several people stood around it, holding onto each other. *What's going on?* Saw asked, but there was no one to hear him or answer.

Later that evening, Jack came into the barn and touched Saw. "Gramps is gone. You and I really do have to have a new partner this winter." Then he leaned against the barn wall and wept, where no one else could see. Finally, he rubbed his face with his shirt sleeve and said (to the ceiling it seemed), "There was so much I still needed to learn from you, Gramps. Why couldn't we have had one more winter cutting together?"

Saw made one trip out of the barn as the leaves turned color—back to the smith for his teeth to be recut in preparation for the winter months ahead. The old smith shook Jack's hand, then pulled him into a hug. "Sorry about your grandfather. He was a good friend."

"Yeah, I miss him."

The old smith took Saw and told Jack to come back in two days.

When the snow flew and covered the ground again, Jack, bag of clothes and blankets on his back, took Saw down from his place and headed out to camp. Other men joined him along the road. Jack recognized one of the branch trimmers from the previous cutting season. They hadn't talked much last winter, but they knew each other from primary school days.

"You got a partner yet?"

"Nope," Jack said.

"How about me?"

"We can give it a go. If it works out, you'll get one third. That's what I got last year. Ought to be fair."

"It's good."

And so, it was agreed. The two walked on together and chose their bunks—the new partner taking the upper bunk and Jack taking the lower.

On the way out in the morning, Saw heard the same words as the previous winter, but this time, spoken by the one-year-under-his-belt sawyer. There were many words the first few days that Saw would not repeat. He wondered if this partnership would survive. Perhaps only their childhood friendship kept Jack trying as he shouted instructions day after day. His most repeated phrase was, "Won't be much for either of us if we don't get our rhythm and saw faster!"

There were a few nights the two young men only glared at each other at dinner. Finally, the new partner learned; things smoothed out; many trees went down. By the end of winter, the two were fast friends and fast sawyers. When the pay was split two-thirds/one-third, Jack said, "Next season, we'll split 50-50."

"Thanks," replied his partner.

Saw returned to his place in the barn for another summer. He was content. Many logging seasons passed in this way.

Jack continued to farm with his parents when each spring came. His grandmother now lived with his parents, and Jack took over the old log cabin and carried his bride across that old threshold. A few years later, Saw could see a little one running around the meadow when the barn door was open.

On one fall trip to town for sharpening, Jack met up with his partner, his partner's wife and their child. "How's this year's catch?" Jack asked.

"Better than last year, but not as good as the years before. Pay's better with you. Don't make much mending trout nets. But we're good."

Year after year went by. But each year, the walk to the lumber camp grew longer. The season came when all the loggers gathered in one place and rode in a large wagon out to the camp.

Jack's children grew up; the oldest, Jack Jr., was expected to follow in his father's footsteps. Saw heard them talking, loudly, as they came to the barn to take him down from his summer resting place. "I don't understand you, Dad! Investing in one of these new hornet saws would be good. They cut faster and better. You want me to learn this, but you refuse to change with the times!"

"Too much money!" Jack shouted. "Can't spend that much of a year's earnings on a damn fancy saw! You know that."

Father and son made it through that winter, but mostly in silence. The talk about the camp that Saw could hear indicated worry over the future of the lumber business. A lot of what they cut now was pulp wood for the paper mill. Stands of white pine were fewer and farther between than ever. Saw heard the roar of the new hornet saw in the distance on a plot of land owned by Foster-Latimer, a new company that had taken over recently. Sometimes, he heard Jack Jr. grumbling with the other men when his father wasn't around. "Think I ought to look for another way to make a living."

Jack Jr. was right. That was the last year for the two of them. It was obvious to Saw that the only thing father and son had in common was their dislike of Foster-Latimer. Both managed to find other work, though, and Saw hung useless in the barn through that winter, and the next, and the next...

Jack Jr.'s cousins, who now farmed the land around the two houses, began to use Saw to cut firewood. Jack Jr. showed them the basics on a few trees so thin in diameter that they didn't need to use wedges, so he never got around to explaining that important step. The small trees they cut fell in whatever direction they wanted, and it didn't seem to matter much.

Then one day, the two young cousins spied a fair-sized maple. "Wow! Let's cut this tree," one said. "Maple is a good hard wood; the logs will burn hot and long in the pot-bellied heat stove!"

Saw wanted to shout, *"No, not without wedges, you young fools! I'll get pinched, sure thing."*

But, of course, he couldn't. The two youngsters sawed away at that maple until Saw was far into the trunk.

And then it happened.

The tree closed itself over the saw, pinched it tight, tight. Try as the two boys might, Saw would not budge. The two were forced to return home for Jack Jr. It was several hours later when they returned.

"You idiots!" Jack Jr. shouted. "Why didn't you put a wedge in?"

"What's a wedge?" the two asked at the same time.

That was when Jack Jr. realized it was his error, because he had never taught them that. He threw up his hands in resignation. "Well, kids, that saw ain't going nowhere ever again. Two-man saws are done for anyway. Just leave it."

Sad, tired, cramped and rejected, Saw sat in the middle of that tree trunk season after season, year after year. He watched small animals and birds climb the tree, sit on the end of him that stuck out. He waited until one day, many years later, a man hiking among smaller, much younger trees came upon him.

"What the heck?" The man began to laugh. Later, he returned with others who also marveled at Saw with the tree growing all around it. The group decided that such an antique would make an interesting display in the Ontonagon County Historical Museum. Together, they decided on a plan to cut the tree above the saw and then below it, but to leave Saw pinched in the tree just as he was. Saw figured it was much better than it had been out in the woods alone.

If you visit the Ontonagon County Historical Museum, 422 River St. in the village of Ontonagon, you can see Saw and many other wonderful pieces of Ontonagon's copper mining and lumbering history.

Please visit www.SupeiorTapestry.com/sites for more info.

Chapter 25 – Daily Happenings at the Ironwood Depot

Fig. 25-1: Ironwood Railroad Depot

This view of the depot is from a postcard around 1910.

Construction on Depot began in 1892. She was built in the style of Richardson Romanesque architecture: baked red brick on a base of Lake Superior sandstone from brownstone quarries near the Apostle Islands and Bayfield, Wisconsin. She had unique features in her three roof lines and decorative trim, which can be seen in the image above. Her slate roof breezeway connected the main part of the depot to a baggage room on the north side. On the rail side, a 400-foot platform ran past the northwest end of the station.

The ground beneath Depot told her that back before the railroad, James "Iron" Wood, the town's namesake, dug a test pit in 1871 to begin the Ashland Iron Mine on the Gogebic Iron Range. In 1882, the even more successful Norrie Mine began when men dug into another part of that iron range. Ground told Depot, "The railroad first arrived in 1884, and you probably remember when they finally incorporated the town in 1899."

"We were all so new," Depot replied. "And how fast the town has grown! I feel like a mother tending to her children."

"Indeed," said Ground. "You sit in the middle of Ironwood supervising a great crossroad. Rails run from here to Ashland, Wisconsin, to transport iron from the Norrie Mine to lake freighters on Lake Superior and from there to steel mills in Illinois, Indiana and Ohio. The Milwaukee, Lake Shore and Western Rail Road, acquired by C&NW RR in 1893, comes to Ironwood and goes south all the way to Chicago, while the Minneapolis, St. Paul and Sault Ste. Marie Railway, the Soo Line, runs east and west. Fredrick Rhinelander, president of the Milwaukee Line, actually rerouted the line so it ran through the Gogebic Range. He had originally intended to go all the way to the Copper Country, but the potential of Gogebic Range and the higher cost changed his mind. There are other railroad lines people could take to reach the copper range."

"So, people considered this a very important stop on the way to Chicago?" Depot asked Ground.

"Absolutely," Ground said. "Ironwood is the largest city on the Gogebic Range!"

Depot was busy throughout the day, since several trains came through at various times. Between trains, the ticket agent, a secretary and a telegrapher were always around. Freight trains kept her busy when they rolled in, needing to unload goods for several retail stores, equipment for the mines, supplies for everyone in town and coal for use in heating and local industries. Then the cars went on a side line to be filled with iron ore, hooked to a different engine and sent north to Ashland and the ore docks there.

But Depot's favorite times of the day came when the passenger trains stopped. Then, she bustled with people, baggage handlers, friends and family greeting arrivals, businessmen needing to go to the hotels and, best of all in Depot's mind, those who arrived on the train coming from Chicago. When the passenger trains arrived, she felt like the town's hostess, greeting new arrivals and making a great impression. She loved to hear the chatter of many different languages: Italian, Finnish, Swedish, Polish, German and many others, in addition to English.

Men who had arrived first, and had saved enough money working in the mine to send ship and train fare to their families back in "the Old Country," kissed their wives and children. Single men arriving without families listened for a sound of their own language, usually an agent of the mining company, who would help them find a boarding house and begin their employment. Depot sometimes heard them say that soon they would greet their wives and children, too.

Women, often exhausted from long journeys across the Atlantic Ocean, followed by the train trip from New York to Chicago and then from Chicago north to Ironwood, often commented on the size and beauty of the town, their new home. "*Ja*, you love it here," husbands would say. "All the candy shops—we get some once in a while for the children; bakeries—I make enough you don't have to make our bread; groceries, too—but I know you still want a garden for good, fresh vegetables. I go saloons sometimes, but I not go often now that you are here. We have house nearby—extra bedroom, so maybe you can take in border, huh? For a bit extra cash."

"I make good soap and lotion," Depot heard one wife say. "Maybe I have my own store sometime?"

"Sure, *ja*, all possible here in America."

Depot loved to hear those dreams, and she watched many of them come true. People worked hard to give their children a better life, and then those children did better than their parents had and later took care of the older generation.

Depot watched as paperboys shouted out the latest edition of the local paper every evening, often selling copies to those getting off the train. She loved the hustle and bustle all around her, day in and day out. Of course, people left town, too, heading east, or west—or down south—once their business was completed. Some headed north, too, where they could change trains to other places.

She watched as contractors and people in the skilled trades built new buildings all around her. While she hated losing that lovely park behind her, the new post office was an impressive building! Depot was shy about introducing herself to Post Office at first, but they did become friends, and she told him all about the town's early days, as

Ground had once told her. He smiled and discussed the many bags of mail arriving on both freight and passenger trains and all the people who came into him to pick up their letters and packages.

Life was so good for Depot that, at first, she didn't notice that gradually, fewer people were arriving. Then, the ore trains didn't run quite as often. In some ways, Depot liked the quieter days, which gave her time to think about everything. In fact, she spent longer and longer times thinking about the busy days of the past. Somehow, she was napping when the mine closed in 1965, because it was no longer profitable to keep digging deeper and deeper for less and less iron ore.

"That is the way with mines," Ground explained later. "The more you take out, the less there is left to mine, until one day, it's all gone, no matter how people thought it would last forever."

In spite of that knowledge, Depot was shocked the day she heard the last ticket agent, Bob Anderson, tell another man that soon, no more passenger trains would run!

What? thought Depot, *What do you mean? No more passenger trains?*

The man with whom Bob spoke had the same reaction, so Bob became specific. "Yup! CN&W let me know that this coming January, the 4th to be exact, will be the last passenger train through here."

The other man shook his head. "I still find it hard to believe after all these years..."

Depot cried that January day in 1971. No more conversations to listen to. No more people coming and going. No more baggage handlers asking if someone needed a ride to a hotel. What was she to do?

True, the freight trains still came through, but the men loading and unloading seldom had time to chit chat. Freight service lasted a little over another decade. Depot knew it was no good to cry that day in 1981 when the last freight train stopped and went on. She resigned herself to her fate, thinking she would probably be torn down.

Depot needn't have worried. The people of Ironwood had not forgotten her or their past. A group of them worked hard to see that on January 14, 1985, Depot would be listed on the National Register of Historic Places. A year later, the City of Ironwood took a chance and bought the building to be the home for the Chamber of Commerce, and a museum. They wrote asking for a grant of $50,000, for total restoration, and received it. The local 400 Club began a fundraising campaign to replace the roof, which was completed in 1987. The names of people who donated were inscribed on bricks in a new walkway at one end.

Now, a street runs between Depot and Post Office where the park once was. She still reminisces with Post Office late at night. She is saddened by the fact that the railroad tracks no longer run behind her, but she does like looking over the newer park on that side, lovely in every season, especially during the summer months. It's often full of people who come into the museum inside her to learn about her past. In her old age, she has come to appreciate the quiet, proud of what once went on around her.

You can visit the Old Depot Museum at 150 N. Lowel, Ironwood, Michigan, 49938. It is open Memorial Day to Labor Day, 12pm to 4pm Mon.-Sat. Winter hours can sometimes be arranged. Phone: 906-932-0287. See www.SuperiorTapestry.com/sites for more info.

Information for this chapter courtesy of Mike Meyer, Chamber of Commerce, and Sandy Sharp, president of Ironwood Historical Society.

Fig. 25-2: Ironwood Depot (2020)

Chapter 26 – Iron Mountain's Monster Pump

From the moment Cornish Steam Pump was installed, he knew his job was important. Any mine that goes down under the ground will eventually go deeper than the water table. Then, water seeps into the tunnels and shaft and must be pumped out if mining is to continue. This has always been true, so it was a constant problem in the copper and iron ranges of Michigan's Upper Peninsula. The Chaplin Mine near Iron Mountain was the wettest of all, possibly the wettest in the entire United States, since it began in what was already a swamp.

The Chaplin Mine Cornish Steam Pump had an ego as big as he was, and he was quick to let every piece of equipment within earshot know it. "None of you could work without me," he often said. "I keep the water out of the Chaplin Mine and it's the biggest producer on the Menominee Range!"

"Yes, we *know*," was the usual reply to Cornish Steam Pump's daily reminders. The other pieces of machinery would have preferred Cornish Steam Pump leave it at that, but, no, he'd always go on.

"I weigh 725 tons, you know! I stand fifty-four feet above the engine room floor, and I'm seventy-five feet from end-to-end. Let's see any of you match that!"

"Huuuummmm, huuuuummmmm," the other working machines would reply, going about their own business.

"And my flywheel is forty feet in diameter. That part of me alone weighs 160 tons. Are you listening?"

"Huuummm, hummm," or, "Sorry, but we are really busy," were their answers.

"You'd all be drowned if I didn't pump 3,190 gallons per minute way down here, where I am 1500 feet below ground! That's 191,000 gallons per hour, or more than four-and-half million gallons per

Fig. 26-1: Chaplin Mine Steam Pump

The restored Chaplin Mine Steam Pump inside his display building.

day...."

One thing was for sure—Cornish Steam Pump knew his math. The other machines droned on, doing their jobs, sometimes amazed that he could talk so much and pump water at the same time. But they *never* told him that.

Cornish Steam Pump also repeated, almost daily, what he had learned from the iron ore coming out of him. What people named the Menominee Range had been found and developed between 1849 and 1851. It was Precambrian Vulcan iron going for miles and miles underground, in some places a mere 300 feet thick and, in others, as much as 800 feet thick. The excellent quality ore was of the hematite and magnetite types and, once forged, became very high quality steel. While Cornish Steam Pump was vital to the Chaplin Mine's operation, all the other machines and men were important, too. Several smaller pumps had taken care of the mine for many years, but Cornish Steam Pump rarely acknowledged them, always claiming all the credit, since he had been installed in 1890.

For many years, he sat in the pump room, 600 feet down in "D" shaft along with other pumps—barely acknowledging their presence and even "forgetting" the fact that he couldn't do his job without the people who kept him running, and constantly refueling his boiler. All Cornish Steam Pump would do was talk about himself and all the water he pumped into huge holding tanks.

He also bragged that he'd been designed by Edwin Reynolds of E.P. Allis Company of Milwaukee, and his nephew, Irving H. Reynolds, and that he cost $250,000—a huge sum at that time. But he downplayed the fact that he hadn't started pumping until Jan. 2, 1893, because it took from 1890 to the spring of 1892 to build him and then more time to haul each huge piece 600 feet down and assemble him for his job. When he did, by chance, acknowledge the other working pumps in place until he started pumping, it was to emphasize that he was bigger and better than those pumps had been.

If the subject ever came up, Cornish Steam Pump blamed the pumps before him for the fact that, beginning in 1885, the Chaplin Mine "settled" due to the amount of ore removed from beneath the City of Iron Mountain forming two large "pits" on either side of Stephenson Avenue. But Cornish Steam Pump would be sure to say that those pits were dry while he was on the job.

Day in, day out, year after year, Cornish Steam Pump worked and worked, keeping the levels and stopes of that great-producing iron mine dry so workers could keep on digging and digging and digging ore to produce steel for a hungry nation growing in industrial power. He never stopped his daily bragging to the other machines, and droning on and on, never tiring as long as men fed fuel into his boilers to keep him running. If he ever stopped or broke down, tunnels would immediately begin to fill with water, draining down from that swampy surface. The fact that mine flooding could happen kept workers very attentive to Cornish Steam Pump, which continued to feed his already-oversized ego.

Unfortunately, the more iron, copper or any metal one takes out of the ground, the less there is left to mine, because there is only a certain amount to begin with—however huge the amount might have seemed. On August 1, 1932, all the workers left the lowest reaches of the mine and went up the shaft, ending their last shift of all time. Those in charge of Cornish Steam Pump shut him down.

"What are you doing?" he yelled. "You can't shut me down! Water will fill the mine. What's going on?"

Silence was the reply. It took a lot less time to dismantle him and dump him on land high enough to stay dry than it had to assemble him where he had worked all those years—perhaps because people needed to get him out of the mine before it filled with water.

Oh, the humiliation!

For once, Cornish Steam Pump remained silent.

He sat that way until 1934, when the Oliver Iron Mining Company offered him to Dickenson County, saying he might be a good "relic for sightseers to visit."

Years later, the Keweenaw Land Association became the holder of the Chaplin Mine land, acquiring it for the mighty sum of $1.00 and tax free, with one provision: the area had to remain fenced. County workers put up a chain link fence, razed the old buildings and cleaned the area. People did come to see Cornish Steam Pump and he did hear words of amazement for his size, but he remained silent in his unused misery. He stayed quiet in 1958 when he was declared a Michigan Historical Site and still quiet when, in 1981, he was placed on the National Historic Site Register. It wasn't until 1984 when people named him a Michigan Historic Civil Engineering Landmark that he began to feel better about himself. But, by then, years of rain, snow, sleet and ice, and the effects of open air, had begun to take their toll on the huge machine.

The Menominee Range Historical Foundation had acquired him in 1982 (or maybe it was 1983; Cornish Steam Pump couldn't remember exactly). They erected a metal building around him to protect him from the elements and preserve him for future generations. Now, he doesn't mind being around other "relics" of his time in his building and in the rest of the museum. He talks with them sometimes at night, apologizing for his earlier behavior. Indeed, he often praises the job they did in working with him "back in the day."

He appreciates the "ooos," "ahhhs" and "wows," he hears from those who see him restored to all his original glory, accepting the compliments cordially with just enough humility to make you like him.

You can visit Cornish Steam Pump at the Menominee Range Historical Museums, 300 Kent St., Iron Mountain, Michigan, 49801 between June 3 and Labor Day. The museum is open from 9-5 Monday through Saturday and from 12-4 on Sunday. Ph. 906-774-4276 or 906-774-1086. Contact Mth-museum@gmail.com or visit www.SuperiorTapestry.com/sites for more info.

.

Chapter 27 – Menominee's Memory: The "Dudly Bug"

Fig. 27-1: Dudly Bug

The last known Dudly Bug as it resides in a museum in California. Perhaps he might be saying that while he has enjoyed his many adventures, he'd like to come home for the rest of his retirement and tell a few stories.

When there are no more "things"—only photographs and fragments of documents of fascinating bits of history—it will be a sad day for humanity. While old photos have stories to tell, somehow, they do not feel so much like characters with personality, lending themselves to the creative juices that flowed through all the other chapters of this book. Such is the case of the inventions of a man named A. Dudly and his sons. A. Dudly was born in Switzerland in 1850. An immigrant to the United States, he ended up in Menominee in 1889.

When Dudly first came to the United States, he settled in Milwaukee, working his trade and finally becoming the foreman at the Kalamazoo Knitting Works of Milwaukee. He was also quite the gymnast, and it was on that account that the Menominee Turner Society recruited him to take charge of their gymnasium. But, in his mind and heart, he loved tinkering with machines. No one can stop an inventive brain.

He started a repair shop for tools and small engines of all kinds and also sold sporting goods and bicycles. However, that did not quite satisfy him, either. As he fixed machines for others, he began to develop manufacturing tools, which earned him several patents. Among these were: the "Perfect Nipple Cup" (1894, for tuning up bicycles), the "Dudly Wheel Turning Stand" (1895), which soon came into wide use all across the country in repair shops and manufacturing facilities and a "Universal Frame Jig" (1897), which was used to construct bicycle frames.

It wasn't long before Mr. Dudly owned a complex of buildings, totaling 6,700 square feet, at the corner of Liberty and Kirby Streets in Menominee. By this time, he also had two sons, Emil and Albert, who worked with him. His bicycles were in high demand as racing bikes all across the country—some advertisements declared that bicycle racers would not ride anything but a Dudly bicycle! Naturally, his factory works contained the most practical machines and tools available—including those he had invented.

Mr. A. Dudly's sons inherited their father's inventive tendencies and were always experimenting with new products for the machine shop to produce. As the automobile age began to expand, their experiments resulted in a rather unusual motor car: the Dudly Bug. It was based on a motorcycle engine and that had a V-belt drive and a two-cycle engine built into a wooden frame. It could carry two people, the driver and one passenger, got forty to fifty miles to the gallon of gas, and reached speeds of thirty to forty miles per hour. The whole thing weighed only 600 pounds! When they had sold

Fig. 27-2: Dudly's workshop

This photo speaks of a busy place, one that was once filled with workers who repaired and built bicycles, a "manly" sort of place. He cannot speak, because not a speck of this building, its walls, its tools, or its workers, remain. Surely, though, there was a camaraderie among the people who worked in this building. How sad must have been the day when the work stopped and everything went away. Did the bricks cry out when they were torn down?

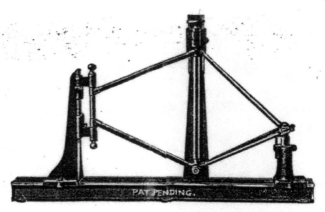

The Universal Frame Jig.

Is especially designed and built for the construction of Bicycle frames. The machine is adjustable in every direction, horizontally and vertically, as well as to the various angles, therefore it will hold and lock a Bicycle frame of any size at any desired angle.

A frame locked in this machine can be drilled and pinned quickly without deranging its correct lines and angles, and after the process of brazing the frame may be placed in the jig again and trued up to positive accuracy.

Particulars and prices on application.

A. Dudly Cycle Works,

MENOMINEE, MICH.

Fig. 27-3: Dudly Universal Frame Jig

Simple looking, but complex in another way, perhaps this tool might say, "I've held hundreds of bicycles in place for repair and manufacture. You should have seen me in my prime and used me to hold a bicycle in place while working on it. I'm an amazing piece of machinery, the product of an inventive mind."

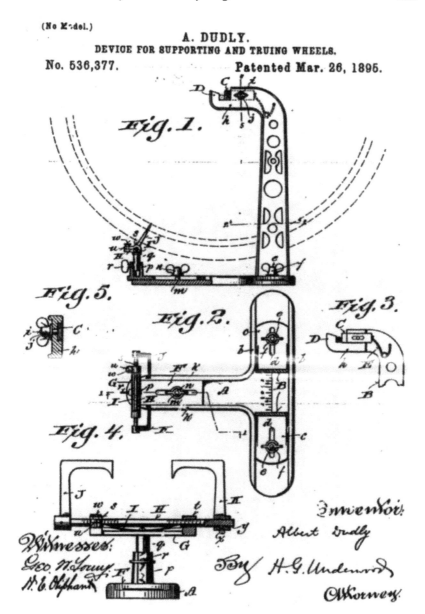

(No Model.)

A. DUDLY.

DEVICE FOR SUPPORTING AND TRUING WHEELS.

No. 536,377. Patented Mar. 26, 1895.

Fig. 27-4: Dudly patent on device for supporting and truing wheels

If this photo could speak, it would tell of the complex measurements, calculations and technical vision of its creator.

"Dudley Bugs" are Being Used In Great European Struggle

"Dudly Bugs," the miniature automobile which is manufactured here by the Dudly Tool company, are playing a prominent part in the Red Cross service on the battle fields of Europe, is can be seen by the use to which one in the above cut is put.

Last spring the above model was originated by the Dudly company and a heavy demand from European purchasers kept the local company busy until the war broke out.

When he saw the above illustration, Harold Tideman, manager of the Dudly Tool company, said: "I knew we shipped some of our output to Germany, but was not aware that they would be used for conveying wounded Germans from the battle fields."

The local company is preparing to double their 1914 output next year despite the war. The machines will be built along lines similar to ordinary automobiles, and instead of the belt drive as can be seen in the illustration, the machine will be propelled by a shaft from the engine.

Fig. 27-5: Dudley bugs are Being Used In Great European Struggle

While the photo and article are grainy and difficult to read, the vehicle in question must have felt proud to be saving lives, rather than killing people.

500 machines of this type, they added a folding top and magneto lights on either side of the radiator. It was reported that one person said that it looked like a praying mantis. A sporty looking bug, it often bounced off roads, which were very rough back then, because it was so lightweight. But that wasn't always a disadvantage. If it was so light and bounced off roads, it was equally light when it came to putting it back on a road. But it was a bit cramped to ride in, so it remained more of a toy of the rich than a serious practical vehicle for the masses.

That light-weight aspect made this specialized vehicle quite useful during World War I. The Dudly brothers knew that they had shipped many of their vehicles to Germany, but they were not aware until later that the vehicles were used to transport wounded men from the front to aid stations and field hospitals. Apparently, they were in wide demand because of their light weight. If the vehicle got bogged down in mud, half a dozen men could simply lift it out and roll it back on its way!

However, the success of the Dudly Bug endeavor did not last. The small business of the Dudly brothers could not compete against better financed, larger automobile makers, especially when, in 1914, Henry Ford offered $50 rebates on his "Model T" if sales of that vehicle exceeded 300,000 vehicles that year. That was the beginning of the end for the Dudly Bug. Sales crashed to nearly nothing. The fad of cycle cars ended abruptly. Few of the vehicles remained in the United States, although many had been shipped to Europe and Asia during the short number of years they were built.

The last known Dudly Bug resides at the Peterson Auto Museum in Los Angeles, California. Not that the City of Menominee wouldn't like to have it back, but to date, resources to purchase the vehicle have not met the asking price. Perhaps with a little more help, and a few more people involved, this piece of Menominee history could be brought back to its birthplace. Then, it could join the one set of tools from the Dudly Bicycle Works, located at the Menominee Heritage Museum and Anuta Research Center.

If we, as a society, are not passionate about preserving the past, many more artifacts in Michigan's Upper Peninsula, and around the country (and even the world), may disappear into dust. Please support the organizations and groups mentioned in all of these stories so that they may survive to inform generations to come.

Information for this chapter was graciously provided by: Menominee County Historical Society and the Spies Public Library.

Menominee County Historical Society
Menominee Heritage Museum & Anuta Research Center
904 11th Ave, Menominee, Michigan 49858
906-863-9000

and:

Spies Public Library
940 1st St, Menominee, Michigan 49858
906-863-3911

Please visit www.SuperiorTapestry.com/sites for links to these organizations and other resources.

Appendix – Resources and for Further Reading

Books, pamphlets, news media:

150 Years, Soo Locks, Harbor House Publications, Boyne City, Michigan, 2005.

Baraga County Historical Society, "History of Casino Gambling in Baraga County", PDF file of a PowerPoint Presentation, and the transcript of the Jan. 30, 2012, "Interview with Fred Dakota", with Russell M. Magnaghi.

Karen A. Brzys, *Superior Land and the Story of Grand Marais, MI,* Gitchi Gumee Agate and History Museum, Grand Marais, Michigan 2016, ISBN 978-0-9760559-1-4.

Fort Wilkins: Yesterday and Today, ISBN 0-935719-69-5, Michigan History Magazine, 2000.

Greg Jaejnig, "The Hearth: heart of the cottage home and family culture", *Daily Mining Gazette* June 6-7, 2020, "Wilderness to frontier did not take long: A fort and cabins were a must," *Daily Mining Gazette,* June 20-21, 2020.

Bernard Lambert, *Shepherd of the Wilderness: A Biography of Bishop Frederic Baraga,* Franciscan Herald Press, 1974.

Larry Lankton, *Cradle to Grave: The Life, Work, and Death at the Lake Superior Copper Mines,* Oxford University Press, 1991, ISBN 0-19-508357 -1.

Gene Meier, *"Askel" Means Step,* The L'anse Sentinel, Palmyra, WI, 1963. Available at the Hanka Homestead Museum.

PDF files: "Why Iron Is Here", "William Austin Burt", "First Open Pit", "Transportation", "Philo Everett", "Men before Machines" downloaded from website: ironheritage.com/history/

Lewis Reimann, *Incredible Seney,* Avery Color Studios, Au Train, Michigan 1982, Library of Congress 81-71825 ISBN 0-932212-26-3.

Quincy Mine Hoist Association, *A Look at the Architecture and Communities of the Quincy Mining Company*, year of publication not listed, no ISBN listed

"Monument to Misguided Enterprise: The Carp River Bloomery Iron Forge", archeological report by David Landon, Patrick Martin, Andrew Seawell, Paul White, Timothy Tumberg, and Jason Menard.

A Return to Honor, pamphlet by the Keweenaw Heritage Society, produced by the society in 2010 and revised in 2014, available only through the Keweenaw Heritage Society for $5.00, which helps with continued maintenance and renovation costs of the Keweenaw Heritage Center.

Bill Rose and Erika Vye with Valerie Martin, *How the Rock Connects Us: A Geoheritage Guide to Michigan's Keweenaw Peninsula and Isle Royale*, Isle Royale and Keweenaw Parks Association, 2017, ISBN 978-0-935289-21-3.

Soo Locks, Sault Ste. Marie, Michigan, U.S. Army Corp of Engineers brochure, Public Affairs Office, 2008.

Regis M. Walling and Rev. N. Daniel Rupp editing and annotating, *The Diary of Bishop Fredric Baraga* ISBN 978-0-814329-99-3, Wane State University Press, Detroit, Michigan, 1990.

Arthur Turner, *Strangers and Sojourners*, Wayne State University Press, 1994 ISBN 978-0-814323-96-0

People

Karen A. Brzys, Grand Marais, Michigan

Jean Ellis, Keweenaw Heritage Center Volunteer

Shirley Donovan Sorrels, Museum of Ojibwa Culture, Saint. Ignace, Michigan

Oscar Heikkinen and Paul Heikkila, Hanka Homestead volunteers

Abbey Hoijer, Curator, Menominee Heritage Museum, Menominee County Historical Society, and Librarian of Spies Library, Menominee, Michigan

Bruce H. Johanson, historian, Ontonagon Michigan

Lynn Johnson, Project Lake Well, expert in Native American cultures of the Great Lakes, projectlakewell@aol.com

Elizabeth Keller, Delta County Historical Society, Escanaba, Michigan, who provided some of the information she had researched for the 150th anniversary celebration of the Sand Point Lighthouse.

Nancy Leonard, Michigan Nature Association volunteer

Karen Lindquist, archivist, Delta County Historical Society

Michael Meyer, Ironwood Chamber of Commerce

Nancy Mannikko, Baraga County Historical Museum volunteer

Elise Nelson, Director of the Carnegie Museum in Houghton, Michigan, information on the Houghton/Hancock Lift Bridge from their collections.

Jean Pemberton, Copper Range Historical Museum, President of the board—summer of 2020, and Karen Johnson, Secretary of the Board—summer of 2020

James Paquette, archeologist and author, Negaunee, Michigan

Carolyn Person, President of the Chippewa County Historical Society

Paul Sabourin, Curator, Sault Historic Site

Sandy Sharp, President Ironwood Historical Society

Websites

A variety of websites including historical societies, museums, historical documents, newspaper articles, videos, and much more can be found on our site http://www.superiortapestry.com/sites

Acknowledgements

We are grateful to the following people and organizations for allowing us permission to reproduce archival or personal photos in *Superior Tapestry*.

Fig. 2-1: St Mary's Rapids: Photo taken by Danny Galarneau, Sault Ste. Marie, Ontario and used with his permission.

Fig. 20-1: *City of Bangor photo* was taken by the author with the permission of the museum board president.

Fig. 25-1: Photo used courtesy of the Ironwood Historical Society, with their permission.

Fig. 26-1: Photo by Mikel Classen and used with his permission.

Fig. 27-1: Dudly Bug: Photo courtesy of the Spies Library in Menominee, Michigan and used with their permission.

Fig2. 27-2, 27-3, and 27-4: All three of these photos provided by the Spies Library, Menominee, Michigan and used with their permission.

Fig. 27-5: The image of the article, with its photo, was supplied by the Spies Library, Menominee, Michigan and used with their permission.

The following chapters originally appeared elsewhere:

A shorter version of "A Tree's Tal" first appeared in the August 2019 issue of *Marquette Monthly*.

"A Stone's Story" was first published in the *UP Reader Volume #4*, the annual anthology of the Upper Peninsula Publishers and Authors Association. See www.UPReader.org.

About the Author

Deborah Kay Olson Frontiera grew up in Lake Linden, Michigan. She taught in Houston public schools from 1985 until 2008 and then taught creative writing part-time for Houston's WITS (Writers In The Schools) program. Upon retirement from teaching, she and her husband moved back to her beloved U.P., but they head south during part of the winter to be with their daughters and grandchildren. She has written for children, young adults and adults, fiction, nonfiction and poetry. Several of her books have won awards.

Visit her websites for more information:
www.authorsden.com/deborahkfrontiera
www.SuperiorTapestry.com

Special offer for readers who visit at least 12 of the sites mentioned in this book:

- Mark the date you visited each place on the logbook (see next page). You may use a photocopy of the logbook to avoid defacing your book.

- Use your phone to take a photo of the logbook and a photo of you or your family at one of the sites. If you can include the book's cover in the shot, that would be much appreciated.

- Email both photos to offer@SuperiorTapestry.com. By mailing you will be giving the author permission to use your photo on her website or social media where other readers can see which sites people have visited.

- Order any book from the author's web site, www.authorsden.com/deborahkfrontiera, and when the autographed book is shipped to you, you will receive a $3.00 refund off your purchase price.

Please note: this offer ONLY applies for orders from the author's web site listed above, NOT Amazon, other web sites, bookstores or gift shops.

My Superior Tapestry Logbook

Date Visited	Superior Tapestry Chapter (Location)
	Birch Bark Canoe
	Bahweting: The Sound of the Rapids
	A Bell Tolls
	Fox River Flowing
	One Piano's Plinking
	Portrait of Pictured Rocks
	Sand Point Lighthouse: A Plumb Assignment
	Ring 'Round the Ages
	A Failure in Forging Iron/ Iron History Museum
	Saturday Sauna/Hanka Homestead
	In Bishop Baraga's Footprints
	Chip of The Pines Casino
	Tools of the Home Speak
	Man Car of Quincy Mine
	A Bridge Across
	The *Lady Be Good*
	A Stone's Story
	At the Corner of 7th and Elm
	Piles of Poor Rock
	Chrysler Calamity on the *City of Bangor*
	A Tree's Tale
	Fireside Stories of Hearth and Home
	Fabulous Float Copper
	Toppling Timber
	Daily Happenings at the Ironwood Depot
	Iron Mountain's Monster Pump
	Menominee's Memory: The Dudley Bug

Index

Aajigade, 13

Anishnaabe, 2, 80, *See* Ojibwa

archaeology, 55–63

Army Corps of Engineers, 17

Ashland, WI, 200

Assinins, 90

Au Sable, 45, 46

B-24, 125–33

Bahweting, 11–17

Baraga, 77, 89–95

Baraga County Historical Museum, 89, 94, 95

Baraga, Bishop, 16, 79–87

basalt, 153–59

Bayfield, WI, 9

Big Bucks Bingo, 92

Brockway, D., 179

Calumet, 73, 135–43, 185

Calumet and Hecla, 155–57

Carnegie Museum of the Keweenaw, 122

Carp River, 65–70, 66, 67, 69, 220

Chaplin Mine, 205–9

Chippewa, 23

City of Bangor, 161–66

City of Cleveland, 85

Civil War, 86, 170, 178, 179

Coast Guard, 52, 53

Copper Harbor, 164, 165, 167–71, 173–80

basalt, 154

copper industry, 16, 46, 75, 83, 105–13, 116–17, 146, 169–70, 174

prospecting, 67

strike, 139

tailings, 153–59

Cornish Steam Pump, 205–9

Cross River, 82

cross-cut saw, 187–97

Dakota, F., 89–95

Delta County Historical Museum, 53

Detroit, 20, 76, 81, 84, 85, 126, 165, 183, 184, 185, 220

Dudly Bug, 211–18

Duluth, MN, 9, 81, 82, 161, 163, 165

Eagle Harbor, 161–66

Eagle Harbor Lighthouse Museum, 161, 166

Edmund Fitzgerald, 19–24

Escanaba, 50, 52

Estivant Pines, 167–72

Fenwick, Bishop, 80

float copper, 154, 181–86

Fort Wilkins Historic State Park, 173–80

Fox River, 25–32

Fresnel lens, 50, 53

Gamble, H., 40

Gay Stamp Mill, 159

geology, 65–70, 176, 183

Gitchi Gumee, 9, 10, 13, 168, 219

Gitchi Gumee Agate and History Museum, 42

Gitchi Gumi Sipe, 11–17

Gogebic Range, 200

Good King Wenceslas, 87

Goulais Bay, 85

Grand Marais, 8, 41, 43, 45–46
  railroad, 30–31, 38–39, 40

Grand Traverse Bay, 159

Hancock, 105–13, 116–22
  basalt, 155

Hanka, H., 71

Harrisville, 85

Harvey, C.T., 16

Hemingway, E., 32

Henry, A., 183

Hiawatha, 45

Homestead Act, 72

Hotel Williams, 46

Houghton, 94, 116–22, 159
  basalt, 155

Houghton County Historical
  Museum, 133

Houghton, D., 183

Hubbell, 159

Iron Mountain, 205–9

Ironwood Railway Depot,
  199–203

Ishpeming, 65–70

Isle Royale, 122, 154

Italian Hall, 111, 145–51

J. F. Schoellkopf, 121

Jackson Mine, 66, 67

Jacobsville sandstone, 43, 65,
  136, 148, 155

Johnson, Lyndon B., 46

KBIC, 92, 94

Keweenaw Bay Indian
  Community. *See* KBIC

Keweenaw National Historical
  Park, 157, 185

Keweenaw Point, 164

Keweenaw Waterway, 117

Kewenaw Heritage Center,
  135–43

L'Anse, 9, 81–82, 87, 177

Lady Be Good, 125–33

Lake Huron, 2, 5, 12, 20, 60,
  80, 85, 162, 163

Lake Linden, 80, 81, 125,
  129, 132, 159

Lake Michigan, 2, 26, 80, 81

Leopoldine Society, 86

Little Bay de Noc, 50

Log Slide Overlook, 47

lumber industry, 27–31, 36,
  75, 170, 187–97
  decline, 40
  shipping, 50

M-28, 25, 26

Mackinac Island, 2, 5

Mackinaw City, 2

Madeline Island, 82

Manistique, 37–38, 40, 81

Manistique Lumbering
  Company, 40

Manistique Railway, 40

Manistique River, 26, 28, 31,
  32, 38

Marji-Gesick, Chief, 66–67

Marquette Regional History
  Center, 63

Marquette Township, 62

McLain St. Park, 117

Menominee, 205–9, 211–18

Menominee Range Historical
  Museums,, 209

Metis, 62

Michigan Iron History
  Museum, 65–70

Michigan Nature Association,
  171, 172

Miner's Falls, 47
Munising, 39, 43–47
Museum of Ojibwa Culture,
  1, 10
Nauitouchsinagoit, 43–47
Negaunee, 65–70
Niagara Falls, 41
Ojibwa, 60, 66–67
  and Bishop Baraga, 79–85
  birch bark canoe, 1–10
  Copper Harbor, 174
  float copper, 182
  Pictured Rocks, 43–47
  Pines Casino, 89–95
  Sault Ste. Marie, 13–16
  spellings, vii
  trees, 167
Ontonagon, 82, 154, 181–86
  lumber industry, 189
Ontonagon County Historical
  Museum, 185, 188, 196,
  197
Ontonagon River, 9, 189
Ottawa, 2, 58, 80, 81
Pictured Rocks, 43–47
Pines Casino, 89–95
poor rock, 153–60
Portage Lake, 108
Portage Lake Lift Bridge, 116–
  22
Quincy Mine, 105–13, 155
Radison, P.E., 44
Red Jacket, 137, 138, 156,
  159, 185, 186
Rese, Fr. F., 80

Sabin Lock, 17, 163
Sable River, 85
Sand Point Lighthouse, 49–54
Sault Ste. Marie, 11–17, 67,
  83–85, 90, 162–63, 179
sauna, 71–77
Schoolcraft, H., 44–45, 183
Selby, H., 179
Seney, 25–32, 33–39, 46
*Societa Italiana di Mutua
  Beneficenza*, 145–51
Soo Line, 200
South Range, 97–103
St. Anne's Church, 135–43
St. Ignace, 2, 80
St. Lawrence River, 6
St. Mary's Rapids, 69
St. Mary's River, 7, 11–17, 83
Superior, WI, 20
Tamarack, 159
Tapiola, 72, 73
watap, 4
Waynaboozhoo, 12, 13
Welland Ship Canal, 41
Wheelus Air Base, 128, 130,
  132
White Pine Mine, 86
Whitefish Point, 8, 21–23, 39,
  163
Willow Run, 126
World War I, 75, 112, 217
World War II, 125–33, 166,
  171
Zug Island, 20

Enjoy Great Stories While Learning More U.P. History!

Michigan's Upper Peninsula is blessed with a treasure trove of storytellers, poets, and historians, all seeking to capture a sense of Yooper Life from settler's days to the far-flung future. Since 2017, the *U.P. Reader* offers a rich collection of their voices that embraces the U.P.'s natural beauty and way of life, along with a few surprises.

You can access any edition of *U.P. Reader* in these formats: paperback, hardcover, eBook, or audiobook (Audible, iTunes).

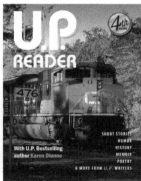
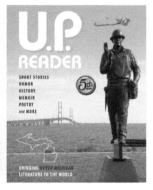